Journey to Resurrection

by John Key

ISBN 0 85346 148 1

Published by
The United Reformed Church
86 Tavistock Place, London WC1H 9RT

Printed by Healeys, Ipswich
Cover and Illustrations by Helen Rogers

Dedication

For Chris
It was unspeakable joy to travel the
pilgrimage of life together for so many years.

INTRODUCTION

John and Christine Key, well loved ministers of Dulwich Grove and Camberwell Green United Reformed churches in South East London, had made great plans for their forthcoming sabbatical. It was to be a pilgrimage. Like pilgrims in all ages, they would visit the holy places of the Christian faith, places where - in T S Elliot's words - prayer has been valid. They had ideas of visiting Santiago de Compostella, Assisi and Rome, as well as places within the British Isles. Much reading and prayer went into the preparation.

Then came the first blow: Christine had cancer. But treatment was possible and there was good hope of recovery. The plans were scaled down but not abandoned. The pilgrimage would be more limited, but would go ahead. Then, a few days before the journey was to start, word came from the doctor that Christine had only a few months to live.

Faith did not falter. The pilgrimage went ahead, but now was even more limited. Both kept intimate diaries during the days of travel and, after Christine's death, John has compiled from both diaries this account of their shared pilgrimage. Those who read it, and I hope they will be many, will be grateful that he has done so.

We all know, with the top of our minds, that we must die. For most of the time we do not take the fact seriously. We live as if there were no horizons. Experience comes to us diluted, spread thinly. John and Christine knew that their life together was to be short, compressed - as it were - into a small compass. This gave a sharpness, a vividness and a poignancy to the ordinary experiences of each day. Small items of daily routine, the taste of a meal, the sight of a flower, the vision of sea and mountain, all had a vividness, a brightness. Each was a special and particular blessing.

All of us live in the presence of death. The time that is given to us is, as a recent Indian Christian writer has put it, a 'space for grace'. When that space is suddenly constricted, everything within it has more solidity, more clarity, more sharpness. Reading this record was - for me at least - a wonderfully fresh re-awakening to the sheer goodness of God in those ordinary things which we take for granted because (in our hearts) we think they will always be there. We take them as part of nature, not as gifts of grace. This very personal narrative will remind us of what they really are.

And there is also something more. The Christian doctrine of divine providence, and the related Christian teaching about prayer and miracle, do not figure largely in contemporary English theology. They have been indeed subjects of mockery by one contemporary theologian who has laughed at Christians who think that God shoots out laser beams every time the believer has a small problem. The record in the following pages is a simple and moving testimony to the Christian experience of answered prayer. Over and over again in small matters and in great, prayer was answered, miracles happened and 'God worked all things together for good'.

I am glad that this very personal record is to be published. Those who read it will, like me, be grateful for the story that it tells and grateful to John Key for sharing it with the rest of us.

Herne Hill
Easter 1995

Lesslie Newbigin

The Author's Family

Dave and Ruth	Son and Daughter-in-law
Sue and Simon	Daughter and Son-in-law
and Matthew	Grandson
Tim and Rebekah	Son and Daughter-in-law
Helen and Andy	Daughter and (now) Fiancé

Other names are explained in the text

JOURNEY TO RESURRECTION

What we see now is like a dim image in a mirror - then we shall see face to face.
What I know now is only partial : then it will be complete.

Meanwhile these three remain; faith, hope and love, and the greatest of these is love.

When the true message, the Good News, first came to you, you heard about the hope it
offers. So your faith and love are based on what you hope for, which is kept safe for you
in heaven.

Colossians 1 and 1 Corinthians:13

Blessed is the one whose strength is in thee, in whose heart
are thy ways
Who going through the vale of misery use it for a well
And the pools are filled with water.

Psalm 84 BCP

It is amazing how when you begin to pray, the coincidences
begin to happen!

William Temple

And a woman spoke, saying, 'Tell us of pain.'
And he said:
Your pain is the breaking of the shell that encloses your understanding.
Even as the stone of the fruit must break, that its heart may stand in the sun, so must you
know pain.
And could you keep your heart in wonder at the daily miracles of your life, your pain
would not seem less wondrous than your joy.
And you would accept the seasons of your heart, even as you have always accepted the
seasons that pass over your fields.
And you would watch with serenity through the winters of your grief.

It is the bitter potion by which the physician within you heals your sick self.
Therefore, trust the physician, and drink his remedy in silence and tranquillity
For his hand, though heavy and hard, is guided by the tender hand of the unseen.
And the cup he brings, though it burn your lips, has been fashioned of the clay which the
Potter has moistened with his own sacred tears.

from The Prophet, Kalil Gibran

FOREWORD

This book is not primarily about illness, death, or bereavement, though these subjects are part of it. It is a simple story of a journey undertaken, as I believe, with a great deal of God's guidance - some felt at the time, some only seen in retrospect. There are a great number of themes in this journey, some planned and some not, and they are woven into one another in a wonderful way that is not of my doing. Some of the themes I have picked out and commented on, but I am aware there are others I have not really pursued.

It has been very difficult to be objective about what happened from my position of partner involved in the journey, but I have tried to understand what was going on in my wife's mind, and wrote much of it from that point of view. Were she here to see what I have written she might disagree strongly with what I have put, but of course I cannot ask her opinion now.

It is just a simple story which I felt worth telling. The value of a story is that it may mean different things to different people: you are able to see it more objectively than I. Naturally it is partly my story, and reflects in some ways my bereaved state at the time of writing, and the way in which the Christian faith speaks to a bereaved person. It was written partly to off-load my feelings, and partly as a record for my family, although primarily to communicate to my many friends what my wife and I experienced together.

St Valentines Day 1995

PART I
PREPARING THE PILGRIMAGE

Prologue

I sat in the summer house on November 3rd 1994, looking out across the countryside to the South Downs. It was a mild, pleasant day, with a hint of sunshine, and the autumn tints were very colourful. I was at a Fairmile Fellowship quiet day at Sayers Common, and I was looking out over a view painted by one of my church members some years ago. As I write this I can see the painting hanging on my wall in my dining room here in Dulwich. As I sat in the summer house, I was thinking back two years - November 3rd 1992. My wife Christine had sat in the same spot then, and had written a prayer. She was also at a quiet day, and was seeking to express her thoughts. She entitled it: "A letter to God, the Maker of Heaven and Earth, and my Maker".

In the letter she wrote: "You have loved me throughout my life - so far - and I know you will continue to do so".

This book is about how God continued to love her over the next 18 months or so, until her death, and how she steadily grew closer to God. People have said to me - "she was very special"; "there was an aura about her"; "there was a warmth that you could feel"; "she brought a light with her into the ward"; "it was something about eye contact, her face, a depth of understanding and love that needed no words".

In the letter she was thinking of some of Mother Julian's writings about expressing love, but in typical down to earth fashion she put in brackets: "(I can't even concentrate too long on this letter without a break - in this case for part of my lunch!)."

Then she wrote, "I need to ask forgiveness every part of every day - a great dark cloud has just temporarily stopped the sun from shining - here at Sayers Common - on a so far beautiful day - and this is like my sin and lack of love. It has just passed over and I feel bathed in sunlight again. My problem is my tongue - a sharpness of words which writes people off in one second - and then I spend time regretting those words.

"From where I sit now, away from the work and pressures of London, I feel bathed in blessings. Thank you God for my family! There are times when I'm sure they have felt second-class - to my church - perhaps even to You. Forgive me for letting them feel like that - because I am too busy - to cook properly - and bake for them. I hope they know how much I love them. They are a constant joy and support to me - and without them (as without you, Lord) I should shrivel up and die. The first frosts of winter would turn me hard and brittle, and then I should fall from the twig - just like the autumn leaves - all around!

"Help me Lord to stay in your love - and theirs. My real family - but also the extended family of the church".

As I sat in that summer house remembering over two years I thought of her 'family' at Camberwell Green where she was minister, and the strain there was for her as she tried to be wife and mother and minister all at once. We both felt it, and I know that it was hard for me to realise that as minister she was independent from me. It was a part of her life not shared with me, that I could only know in snatches, as a husband on the sidelines. It took it out of her -

the worry about people moving away, the jobs to be done by so few people, the faithful attendance at worship Sunday by Sunday even when she wasn't preaching. Camberwell Green was part of her special family - as were patients at King's College Hospital where she was free church chaplain. A fellow chaplain wrote to me, "Christine was not only a tremendously valued member of the chaplaincy team but a good friend as well. Her quiet manner, deep faith, immense pastoral sensitivity and genuine love and empathy for the patients she visited, as well as her support for the rest of the team, will be sorely missed. In my work I have over the years encountered numerous chaplains of various denominations including my own, and I can genuinely say that Christine ranked as one of the finest I have had the privilege to serve alongside". This was another part of her life I could not share - just be the taxi-man dropping her off with her bag holding the communion set, the bible, the prayer books and the cards with good wishes for healing and wholeness.

There was tension and stress, we were both so busy and time for each other and the family was limited. And when we did go out together for a day, the troubles of Camberwell Green would surface, my work at Dulwich Grove would come up, and we'd look for support from each other in our work, and very often we were both too tired to give it.

So she went off to Sayers Common without me, to recharge her spiritual batteries in quiet reflection. As she sat in that summerhouse, behind the beautiful oast-house shaped chapel of the Franciscan community there, her thoughts turned to me, and what I was doing that day.

She wrote, "I'm in a summer house - a little wooden building - have only been disturbed here twice - and another "wooden house of retreat" is probably having its fate decided at this very moment! Lord, only You can make that final decision - and we shall have to abide by it!! I leave that in Your hands. There are the rising hills of the South Downs here in the distance - but a barbed wire fence is separating us from them! Please don't let my tongue be a barrier to anyone!" "I leave that in your hands".

Strange that two years later to the day I was attending a quiet day taken by Kate Compston about "In God's hands and ours", and that she quoted a poem that Chris placed in our "wooden house of retreat": "I said to the man who stood at the gate of the year 'Give me a light that I may tread safely into the unknown'. And he replied 'Go out into the darkness and put your hand into the hand of God. That shall be to you better than light and safer than a known way'".

God's hands were about to shape our lives in a way we could not anticipate. We were going forward into the dark unknown on a journey that had God's hand upon it. And before we knew what was about to hit us, he was already leading us to take decisions that would help to make that journey not only bearable, but very wonderful for both of us. Kate Compston spoke of Rodin's sculpture of the hand of God encompassing the human form with that form stretching out, supported by God's hand, to be itself, to realise its full potential. That, I am sure, was God's hand for us, giving us a base, a foundation, on which to build a pilgrimage to life and death and resurrection. Without those first decisions we made that we felt were somehow God's guidance and plan, the rest could not have happened, but they were made in total ignorance that Chris was about to suffer from terminal cancer that would cause her death in July 1994.

The Cottage

One of these plans concerned 'the wooden house of retreat' and rested upon the visit I was making that day, November 3rd 1992, to my father in Mill Hill, London. He was about to make a big decision about a loan to me, and was not really prepared to make it till a letter arrived. November 3rd came, the appointed day, but there was no letter. I 'phoned him and he felt he was not ready, but wanted me to go and see him as planned anyway. As I was putting on my coat to set out, a letter plopped through the door - a blue air letter. I turned it over. Yes, it was from my brother, Geoffrey, on holiday in Australia. He had sent it not realising its importance or urgency, in response to one I had sent, in hope that it would find him. He had left a number of addresses, but his itinerary was not totally fixed. I passed the letter over to my father, who found decisions very difficult to make, especially where large amounts of money were involved. He read and re-read the letter - and then looked up with a smile. He said, "Shall we go to the bank now, John?". And I think both he and I knew God's hand was in the decision, for the letter arriving just then was more than a coincidence. But we did not know why.

Now I must tell you the whole story of the 'wooden house of retreat' and why a decision had to be made that day.

Vera Todd, a church member, died suddenly of a stroke on April 7th 1992. She was about to go with a friend to her beloved cottage in Sedlescombe, which she had owned as a holiday home for nearly 25 years. Many people in Dulwich Grove church know the cottage well. They had stayed there for holidays or gone down for days. At first the cottage and garden were well cared for and well used and a source of great delight to Vera, but latterly as she got older it had got neglected a bit, as I saw when I had gone the autumn before .

After her funeral Dulwich Grove learnt that Vera had left the cottage to the church, and that the terms of the will were such that it could be kept for the church's use, or sold and the money used for any purpose the church felt right. Though Vera had suggested that people, including the minister, should be able to have holidays in it, it was felt the upkeep of a property so far from London (Sedlescombe is near Hastings) would be too difficult. The church meeting agreed to sell the cottage and use the proceeds for the purchase of a property in East Dulwich to rent to a family in housing need.

That summer, in August, Chris and I were able to go with my aunt to stay three nights at the cottage as part of our holiday. It was damp and a bit chilly, but both of us fell in love with the place, and we all had a lovely time. We were sad to give the key back, but soon we were off to Wales and Ireland, to visit places we had not been to since our honeymoon - a wet, nostalgic, but beautiful holiday - but that's another story. When we got back it wasn't long before Chris said, "Can we go to the cottage again?", but it was up for sale, the keys were at the estate agents, and that was the end of that. We felt very sad, but knew there was nothing we could do about it.

One day the idea came. How about asking my father for part of my inheritance? We made some suggestions in a light-hearted way - then more seriously. We talked with David, our church treasurer. We counted up our money, including what Chris had inherited from her parents. Then there were the questions. What is our motivation for doing this? When you live in a tied house, such as a manse, you feel insecure as you grow towards retirement. To have a little place of your own gives you security. I talked with URC retirement housing, and they were not enthusiastic - saying that with a wooden building there could be no help at retirement to extend or modify, but that we could buy it and sell it in five or six years time when there could be help with capital to buy a brick built place. Oh, well, it was a nice idea ...

Then there was the idea of helping a homeless family in Dulwich - no one was buying, the housing market was dead - it would move things along for the church to get the money to buy a property. That idea appealed strongly, and some people told me now was the time to buy: the housing market would soon recover and it would be a good investment for later. I had enough capitalism in me to be attracted by this argument, but Chris was unimpressed.

She said simply, "I love the place, and I believe God wants us to buy it". We left it for a while but it wouldn't go away, and I initiated a house survey, and then made a tentative offer. It was a strange situation, buying from the church, even though estate agents were involved. It was necessary to get Dad to say definitely "yes" or "no", after he had agreed in principle that it was a good thing to do. I agreed to make a firm offer on November 3rd and that was what I was doing when Chris was at Sayers Common writing her prayer. So the hand of God guided us - we believed. Our pilgrimage together would not have been possible without Brickwall Cottage. Our family were not impressed when we took them to see it one January day. The sun was out but it was frosty. We put the fire on but it didn't touch the place. There was an icicle hanging from the tap in the kitchen, the front door was swollen with damp and needed all our strength to get it open, there was mildew on the chairs, rot by the kitchen door, and one outside wall was green with mouldy stuff. Fortunately we had taken Dad on a warmer day in the autumn!

But to us it was right. The Dulwich Grove folk were thrilled the cottage would be still 'in the family' as it were. Beauty and contentment stemmed from its history and from its position in the beautiful village. It was hidden yet convenient, and the stress of our busy lives would fall away for a time. It was a 'wooden house of retreat' that we needed in order to survive the strain of everyday living, and be close to one another for a while.

So we got excited, waiting the three months for Dad's money to be available. I read all about Sedlescombe's history and we discovered it had been the gardener's cottage for the Brickwall House, now the Hotel, next door. Chris had plans for things in the house - curtains, carpets, pictures. But we hadn't much time to dream - we were both so busy.

The Sabbatical

The second part of God's plan came quite out of the blue. I was contacted by Michael Rees, President of the Bromley District of the URC, to say my name had been put forward by the General Purposes Committee as the next District President. It was a two year appointment beginning in June 1994. This was mid-January 1993. I was quite amazed. I wasn't even on any district committee. I felt quite inadequate to do the job, but Chris was very encouraging. "If they've asked you to do it, they must think you can", she said. Of course I had been district secretary in Birmingham, but not for long.

I thought about it for a while, and then realised I was due for a sabbatical in 1995 and couldn't take it while I was president. Maybe I could take it a year early? I made enquiries and it seemed as if it could be possible. I put it to the church and they agreed that February-May 1994 would be far enough away to make necessary arrangements, and close enough to fit it in before I took office. And, although the sale hadn't gone through yet, maybe we could stay at the cottage for part of it? I rang Michael back and said yes, I would do it if the district agreed. I booked the Sabbatical with the church - it was a year away, but plans had to be started.

In February 1993 everything suddenly happened. On the 8th we went to my Dad's to arrange for his money to go into my account, and we had agreed to sign the contract for the cottage on the 16th, which we did. There was no going back at this stage very easily - nor did we want to - but on the 11th Chris found the lump in her breast. It had been hurting her a bit for a day or two, and that evening she had found it while I was out at a meeting. The next day we went to the doctor - he was noncommittal but referred us to King's College Hospital, for a test. Christine had had a lump before which had been removed and was found to be benign.

At this stage there were four things on our minds - the purchase of the cottage, the presidency, the consequent sabbatical, and the lump. The first three could be connected - the sabbatical partly based at the cottage, but we did not dream that these two would be intimately connected with that little painful lump. It was all in God's hands, and in some way God wove it together, but I do not believe God sent that lump, even if he foresaw it. At this period, Chris went to the Fairmile Fellowship three day retreat starting on Shrove Tuesday, and I had a church meeting where we all had pancakes. On Ash Wednesday I went to the cottage to work in the garden and clear the furniture for the wood preservative man to come and treat the floor and roof for woodworm. But Chris's mind was on other things at the retreat as she recalls in her diary which she wrote a year later on our pilgrimage.

She says: "I guess for me it (the pilgrimage) started almost a year ago now. Just before the Fairmile Fellowship I had found the lump in my breast. We had 'Ashing' as it was a Lenten Iona retreat. 'Ashes to ashes - and to dust we shall return.' It was based on a phrase of George MacLeod, from his book 'The Whole Earth Shall Cry Glory'; and this began to prepare me for my Way of Pilgrimage - ('In the garden also, always the thorn') Some of the headings were - 'What's in the cupboard? a time to check on our reserves and a time of emptying!', 'Fierce floods of tears' came next an honest look as we go from wilderness with Christ to garden'. We all affirmed our baptism (and I've been doing that a lot just recently!). We finished up with a Communion Service on the theme 'The Wedding Garment of Rejoicing' - What a glorious future hope we all have if we are in Christ. Someone complained it was all too heavy and sad! But I suspect she wasn't coming to terms with real life!".

So even at this stage Chris and I were diverging: I was full of plans for the future, and she was coming to terms with what was happening within herself. Both were part of the preparation for the pilgrimage - hers probably much more spiritual than mine. But it was a very long time before we would realise that the sabbatical / pilgrimage would coincide with her journey to death - indeed it was another year yet before we knew.

Planning the Sabbatical

It was pretty soon after we had agreed the Sabbatical should be February to May 1994 that we realised it was very easy to make it combine with the start of Lent, with February 16th being Ash Wednesday, and end with Pentecost Sunday on May 22nd. So I would preach on February 13th, and there would be a 'send-off' for us that day, and I would preach on Pentecost Sunday as my first Sunday back. I had been reading Father Gerard Hughes *'In Search of a Way'* and suggested that Pilgrimage should be our theme. As he had gone to a deserted island near Iona, and then to Rome, I suggested perhaps we could go to Rome and Iona. I was concerned that the journey itself should be important, not just where the journey went to - in the same way as the pilgrimage around Iona each week takes on meaning at the various stages on the way - and the leader seeks to interpret the stops in a spiritual way. The journey through Lent leads to Easter, but Easter is not the point of Lent. Lent stands on its own, but also takes on the role of a spiritual journey to Easter. A pilgrimage may or my not lead to a great climax of arriving at somewhere special at the end.

Chris had ideas of a pilgrimage through Europe to Rome and Assisi, calling at friends on the way in Holland, Germany, and Milan where we might perhaps stay for a while. The idea of Assisi came from our knowing Sister Joyce at King's College Hospital who is a Franciscan. I had ideas of walking part of the Pilgrim Way to Canterbury in Kent and Sussex using the cottage as a base. We thought of pilgrimages to Glastonbury and Walsingham, or a 'William Carey tour' like one advertised in a holiday brochure. We thought of going to Wales and exploring the Saints' road to Bardsey in the Nevin area where we've had such lovely holidays in the past. We thought of going to Israel and Lourdes, perhaps in connection with a visit to Rome. At the Horniman museum there was an exhibition about the Pilgrimage to the shrine of St James at Santiago de Compostella. We had a long talk with Alan Fox at the Christian Education Centre in Crawley, who is very much into pilgrimages, and it was in one of the books he showed us that I read about someone starting a pilgrimage at Callanish in the Hebrides.

Eventually we fixed a few dates. We booked to go to the Fairmile retreat in February and the Ministers and Spouses conference at Eastbourne in March. We felt it would be good to be at Iona on Easter Day. We also booked a modified package deal to go to Rome and Assisi from 21st February to 7th March. And maybe we could go from Iona to the Hebrides and see Callanish and stay with our friends who live nearby.

There was a lot of thought given to the reason for the pilgrimage, and what its spiritual purpose was. The mediaeval pilgrimage was to gain a place in heaven - a once in a lifetime thing to do to earn grace. This was obviously not for us, but there was always the feeling of purpose behind it, a spiritual living for three months to gain greater spiritual insight, as Father Gerard Hughes had used his pilgrimages to practise the spiritual exercises of St Ignatius.

Eventually we costed it all out, as far as we had planned it, and applied for grants. Chris got a grant for in service training as Non-Stipendiary ministers do not get sabbaticals, and I got the full grant available for a Sabbatical. All this planning took a great deal of time over a long period, but it was by no means all the preparation we did. It must be remembered that much of it was done with the backdrop of Chris's cancer and medical treatment.

Preparing the Cottage

We had never been into house purchase before and it was exciting but a bit daunting. The initial survey pointed out some minor things that needed doing, but there were warnings in it that wooden structures would need more upkeep than a conventional brick structure, and that carpets and furniture had prevented a thorough examination of the floor, and that without demolishing the building it was impossible to see the main wall structure. There were some ominous signs - the lovely wooden seat in the garden fell apart with rot when we sat on it - the garden gate was very rickety and eventually fell apart too - as did one of the handrails up the steps. The solicitor told us it might be difficult to get insurance on the place because it was wooden - but in fact there was no problem - and he, too, warned us about the problems of wooden buildings. We were fortunate that the sale was through the church, and we were allowed access before the final completion date. The first thing was the wood treatment, and while Chris was at Fairmile Court with the ashing ceremony already referred to, I was at the cottage trying to clear furniture and carpets so that the floor and roof could be treated for woodworm, and while they were doing it they could inspect under the floor for any rot. The carpets were really damp, and needed throwing out; the old saggy bed likewise, and a dressing table had woodworm in it and had to go too. During my efforts a wardrobe fell over onto its mirror, but was caught by the bed frame - no harm done - I was so relieved. The bathroom and kitchen were piled high with furniture - so from then on for a while we had to use the loo down the road by the car park! Then the men came to do the timber treatment, and I waited for the telephone to ring to say they'd found rot - but it didn't, and eventually the report was fine, and they'd taken all the rubbish with them too! The next thing was stripping the bedroom walls and painting them. We went to the Links, Eastbourne, for the Ministers and Spouses conference, 1993, and the afternoons were free, so all that week we spent these afternoons at the cottage, getting away immediately after lunch, and arriving back just in time for evening dinner. By this time Chris knew the breast tumour was malignant and had some pain with it, and the drugs they were giving her made her feel weak. But we worked together removing soggy paper and then painting. We had heating on and windows open. Fortunately the weather was lovely and sunny, although only March. The wood treatment was water based so things were even damper. Without that conference in Eastbourne as a base, there was no way we could have done it, and we worked so hard, fighting against time. But at the end of the week it was all done - not professional, but quite adequate - and we had ordered carpet from Eastbourne for the two bedrooms and the large living room. During the conference there had been the Budget, and as a result we didn't have to pay stamp duty on the house purchase, so we could spend more on carpets and curtains. Things were working out.

So we went to Lewisham and ordered the curtains, and the new double bed. It was lovely to have a project to be getting on with, as we had something to take our minds off the cancer, and all the hospital visits. In Chris's diary for Monday, March 29th she has: "To Sedlescombe for carpet delivery 4.30 pm. Primroses and Big Snowdrops", and then on the Friday of that week, "Completion date for cottage - Sue and Simon and Matthew for the day, but they couldn't come because of my radiation". (It was a bone X-ray test). Then the next day, Saturday, "Curtains and four cushion covers. Coffee morning. Prepare for Easter".

The following Monday Tim came for a couple of days - there was Breast Assessment Unit in the morning and we were at the cottage afterwards laying carpets (Tim was a great help). Everything had to be done on one day visits as there was nowhere to sleep. We still couldn't use the kitchen or bathroom until the carpets were down and the furniture could be moved. Thank goodness for the loo in the car park! But now at least we didn't have to go to the estate agents to borrow the key, the place was ours, and the following week (after Easter Sunday) we went off on the Tuesday to spend our first week living at our beloved cottage. Chris packed the car up to the roof with all the things we would need. She didn't realise then, but Easter Sunday 1993 was to be the last service she took at Camberwell Green.

Everything worked very well. The plumber arrived to get the airlocks out of the pipes - the system had been drained, of course - and fixed the valve upstairs so that it didn't bang away every time we turned the tap on. The bed arrived on time, and fitted in the room beautifully. The curtains all fitted. The coal fire burned brightly - didn't smoke at all. The storage heaters worked (we hadn't been able to test them before). The whole week was quite trouble-free, and although there was a lot of work to do, we had lots of trips out as well, our first holiday at this lovely place. We knew somehow it was all meant to be. If anything had gone wrong we couldn't have coped with all our responsibilities at our churches over Easter and with frequent visits to the hospital clinics with Chris. It was a very tight schedule, but now it was habitable. My headache about where to put the car was solved, as the Brickwall Hotel owner was prepared to give me a space on his car park for the week, and eventually was persuaded to let me keep it indefinitely.

The day we came back the Bromley URC district council meeting in Beckenham voted for me to be the next president. In my speech of acceptance I told them as much as I knew of Chris's illness, and asked for prayers for both of us. Everyone was very sympathetic and it was the beginning of feeling uplifted in prayer by so many people. From this time on we never sought to hide what was wrong from anyone. And although we were so worried, the cottage was a real comfort. It was always there to run to, the stress always melted away when we got there - it lived up to and exceeded all our expectations. It was a little bit of paradise in a world of pain and nightmare.

The Cancer and the Medical Treatment

I would like to say at the outset that in hindsight I have no criticism whatever of the treatment given to Chris by King's College Hospital. The staff were superb, understanding, patient and helpful. We got to have a really good relationship with them, and they gave us such a lot of their time. Chris was able to do a bit of 'pastoral caring' as she waited for her treatment, and worked out some of her chaplaincy duties in the gaps between treatment. So many people seemed to know her, and they all loved her. She remained cheerful most of the time - at least outwardly - and managed to raise a smile from most of the patients she talked to. There was a lot of talk about the symptoms, the effect of the drugs, what the doctor said, etc., but also talk of lots of other brighter subjects, and when she got home she was full of stories of other people. Very often we went together for the consultations, and were able to share fully in what was happening, but of course she went on her own to the treatments so I only had her description of what it was like.

Things could have been done differently, of course. Operations could have been done, but the cancer was so active that I think the outcome would have been the same, and she would have had a lot of hospitalisation. In the way it was done, her quality of life remained good all through. It is quite possible an operation might have accelerated and spread the cancer, and brought her a lot of pain and an earlier death. Who knows? What we learnt in those clinics was that no two people are the same, and that the experts are more likely to make the right decisions. Chris once said to her consultant, "How do you cope, breaking bad news to people so often?" and she replied, "There are a lot of people praying for me all the time". It was such a comfort to know that, and we prayed for her too - she looked so tired and drawn that day, not her usual strong smile of encouragement. Cancer is a rotten thing to deal with day after day - thank goodness for people strong enough not to let it get them down.

What I say here may seem like criticism at times, but it isn't. I am trying to reflect our moods, our frustration, our fear and anxiety and the nightmare quality of some of the time.

When Chris found the lump we immediately made an appointment with the local GP. He examined her - confirmed it was something that needed investigation at a hospital - and wrote a note to King's. He said an appointment would take about a fortnight to come through. We wanted him to say he thought it was nothing serious, but he said he could give no guarantee. In due course there was an X-ray and a biopsy done. Then the appointment to get the result. During this time people sought to reassure us. "It's only a fatty lump - lots of people get them"; "She had one before, didn't she? That was fine"; "Nothing to worry about, John"; "Look on the bright side, don't look so anxious". I'm afraid those well meaning remarks were not helpful. I wanted to say, "What happens if it is cancer?" - but I knew I was crossing the bridge before I got there. But why did the lump hurt if it was benign? As it was, I felt very unprepared when at last I saw Chris emerging from the clinic after waiting an hour longer than I'd expected. Her face gave it away. She'd had to wait ages before someone came and said, "Has anyone told you?" We sat and had a coffee and tried to take it in. Such things only happen to other people. Then there were drugs to get, a blood test to do, and more appointments to fix. It was like a nightmare, and we wanted to wake up and find it wasn't true. Then there were 'phone calls to everyone to tell them. So many people were waiting on that result.

Still, it all seemed pretty straightforward - take the tamoxifen, it will shrink the lump, and then an operation - a partial or complete mastectomy and hopefully all will be well. But it all took so long. And there was Chris saying, "No, not that week, we're on holiday - no, that's the ministers and spouses conference", whilst I was inwardly saying, "Chris, don't delay, your life's at stake". But whose life was it? Already, perhaps, she was thinking - "I want to live, not exist at medical consultations". I was selfishly wanting to preserve her life because I didn't feel I could live without her.

Tamoxifen is not a pleasant drug to take and many people have nasty side effects. Fortunately Chris could cope with it, which was just as well, as she took it regularly for over a year, together with the blood pressure tablets, and quantities of neurofen which she took for her stiff muscles and headaches she'd had for a number of years. No one would have guessed how many different tablets she was taking when she put on her smile and she never said a word about it to most people.

But then came warnings of things to come - the tamoxifen was not shrinking the lump. It was a bit like an octopus in shape with lots of tentacles . They felt a lump in her neck and looked worried. Chris got sensations in the lump, like bees stinging her and they decided to do an operation. We said to each other, "Why don't they get on and operate on the lump before it grows too big". Still, we supposed, they knew best.

We had some time at the cottage after Easter - our first week there. Chris cancelled her next few Sundays at Camberwell Green to have a short holiday, then the neck operation, and finally the mastectomy. We rang the hospital on the day of the operation - no bed - rang at lunchtime - still no bed - rang at 4 pm - it's been cancelled. I was very annoyed - yet more delay - so I rang someone in the clinic who was very annoyed too. "It's all fixed", she said, "the surgeon, the operating theatre". She worked some magic, and Chris was in the private ward by 7 pm - as an NHS patient, of course. All went well, and soon she was home, having had wonderful private food and treatment, and making the most of it!

However there was another worry - one of the doctors was concerned about a red patch on her breast by the lump putting it down to bruising after yet another biopsy. We went back later for the consultation. It wasn't our consultant, but a more junior doctor. "Yes", he said, "the neck is fine - no evidence of cancer there - but what's that red patch - and the lump is bigger". (They kept getting out instruments to measure it) He got another consultant to look, and she appeared very worried. They prescribed a strong antibiotic in case it was just an infection, but both agreed a mastectomy was not possible with it like that. In answer to questions about alternatives, we were told probably chemotherapy was the best, but a decision would be made the following week by the consultant.

Chris went through agonies with that antibiotic. Helen had come home early from Romania (where she'd been through enough looking after the AIDS children, watching one after another die) because she was worried about her Mum. It was about this time Chris had to stop wearing a bra - it hurt too much. She hated the speed bumps in the road because the jolting hurt her. At the back of our minds we thought of a friend in Birmingham who died of breast cancer which had spread up her neck and down her arm. If only they had operated sooner. Why did they delay? What agonies was Chris going to suffer? She showed the lump to me. It was red and angry. "I'm sure it's bigger than yesterday", she said, and we were very scared. One of the terrible things about cancer is that it produces fear. It gets hold of people and pushes them down into the dark, taking hold of their lives, as well as their bodies. It was a long, bad week and just thinking about it starts my heart racing again. Thank goodness Helen was there to help us through.

Eventually we were back at the clinic to find it was all fixed for the first chemotherapy treatment that day. It would be the strongest sort. Chris would lose her hair, and she was told where to get a wig. We **did** have a choice about the treatment - we could say no! There were to be four sessions, one every three weeks, over a period of three months. That took us nearly up to Tim's wedding. After 6 weeks they'd be able to tell if the treatment was working - possibly after three. There was a great load of tablets to take on top of all the others. After the treatment Chris was advised to go straight home and lie down, but she wanted to get the tablets, have the blood test, and have something to drink - strong coffee preferably. We staggered round the hospital, but eventually she had to give in and get home and go to bed, although not before she'd talked to lots of folk including the chaplains. She recovered after a couple of days and found a positive effect. "My muscle pains I've had for so long have gone", she said. They never came back - no more neurofen. Maybe this was a turning point.

Fighting Back

People sent get well cards, people 'phoned, lots and lots of prayer groups put Chris on their list, and Chris said with a smile, "The bees have stopped stinging me". But it was hard to go to the wig shop. What sort of thing would it be? Chris was not keen, but Helen was very encouraging. "Match it up with what you have now and it won't be too bad", she said. Chris looked at the catalogue - decided which style, and said to me, "You can buy it for me for my birthday, John". I protested that it was hardly a birthday present, but she insisted. So we went. When the girl got it out - all funny curls - it looked awful, but she gave it a shake, put it on Chris, and Helen and I said immediately: "That's it - it's just right". It was such a relief. She wore it that Sunday over her real hair, and lots of folk didn't realise for it just looked as if she'd been to the hairdressers. She never pretended. When people said, "I like your hair" which they often did, she always told them, but she was really pleased. She was able to live a normal life, and it made all the difference in the world. But she hated having to wear it. It was hot, it threatened to blow off in the wind, and she had to be careful to get it on right - not too far forward or back - and to cover up the hairline with wispy bits so that it didn't show. But we had fun with it too. "Keep your hair on Grandma!" had a different ring to it! Matthew was intrigued to see it hanging on a hook, for she preferred to wear a headscarf when she was with the family.

The worst thing was when the hair was coming out. A friend, Charlotte, came. She had a chat and described how her hair had come out, sometimes in great clumps. With Chris the comb was full of hair; the waste paper basket was half full some days, it was all over the carpet and in the bath. At first it just looked thinner, then bald patches appeared and then it had all gone apart from a few wisps right at the back. First she wore a hairnet in bed, then a woolly hat. She always apologised to me if I was in the room when she uncovered her head. It was a shock to see her like that, and I always tried to respect her privacy. But we could live with it, and between chemotherapy sessions she felt quite comfortable and the wig just became part of life. That first six weeks were reasonable - the aches and pains had gone, the breast was less painful. She wrote on a piece of paper I found later: "Can I offer as far ahead as Nov-Dec to take communion at Camberwell Green? I have to feel a lot more confident than at present. I need to have the energy and the concentration - I need to have a 'Word from the Lord' - to make up for all these weeks and months of silence! Remember you are feeling at your very best just before the next chemo!! and that is when you wrote this down!!"

Just before the third chemotherapy treatment her consultant examined her, and we got a shock. "Oh dear", she said "That's not doing any good". We were taken aback - it had felt better, and the sore patch had looked a bit better. The treatment had stopped it growing, but that was all. So the next two treatments were a different type. I read in the consultant's eyes she wasn't very hopeful, but said nothing to Chris. If it didn't work there was always radiotherapy, she told us - and said 20% or so of cancers were chemo-resistant. The fear began to come back for me, but Chris was working at how to fight cancer in a different way, through attitude and mental imagery, reading books about it. She has always been a great reader about psychology and spiritual attitudes. When she had her babies she did it by the book *'Babies without tears'*. Relaxation, breathing - lots of people do it now, but not then. Now she was into *'Getting Well Again'* - an American book, which says on the cover "The Bestseller about the Simenton's Revolutionary Life Saving Self Awareness Techniques". It was her 'bible' for a while, lent to her by Charlotte, who had found it helpful. There is a lot in it about mental imagery, thinking in a positive way about your body getting better and destroying and flushing out the cancer cells. You have to read the book to understand it properly, but it certainly changed her whole attitude. The fear was going and there was a fight, a determination. She once said to me, "I'm going to beat this bugger if it's the last thing I do". We had been giving in to the fear -

the cancer was having it all its own way. Things had changed, and we were no longer going to let it control our lives. We were going to live. And if ... well, we've all got to die sometime. If you turn and face death head-on, all its power disappears.

Chris got there long before I did. She was already setting goals to achieve. The most important one was Tim's wedding. Tim and Rebekah had asked her to take their wedding earlier. It was to be in Manchester, and lots of people were to be there and about half the guests seemed to be ministers. It wasn't so much whether Chris would be well enough to get there, but that the treatment seemed to leave her very emotional and anything like that would probably set her off crying, or her voice would break up and she wouldn't be able to do it. A stand-in was organised who would be there anyway, the college chaplain, but she would only do it in extreme emergency. It was important for Chris, and for Tim and Rebekah, that it would go as planned.

The medical situation was not good. The following two chemotherapies had had little or no effect. The radiotherapy could not be started immediately as the effects of the chemotherapy had to be allowed to wear off first. The 'bees' came back again. She showed it to me - it was big and angry, deforming the breast considerably, almost as big as a tennis ball, and each day it looked larger. However, she <u>was</u> going to the wedding, and having a holiday after as planned. Death was staring her in the face, but the radiotherapy was put off for the wedding and the holiday. The cancer was put in its rightful place, non-urgent compared with living.

She was free of treatment for a while and making the most of it, a leisurely trip up to Manchester, a night staying with our Egyptian doctor friend at Stoke on Trent and then up to meet the family, gathering from different places. She was all smiles, enjoying every minute. She joined in all the family fun and it wasn't an act - she was really happy. And the next day at the wedding she did her part perfectly, not a quiver in her voice till she pronounced them husband and wife - and then it was so natural, what mother wouldn't? She looked radiant in her lovely stole, as if she'd been taking services regularly for the last four months, rather than having operations and chemotherapy. She played with the children, and talked to the guests, and knew everyone as she always did - helping me out with names and faces as usual. No-one knew that in her diary she had put in faith 'A Goal' beside the date. Ina and Andreas, our German friends who were at Tim's wedding, would get married the following year, but only I was there. In her diary she had put 'A Goal' beside that date too, but it was not to be. The following week, on our holiday, my brother took a photo of us at the top of the steps of our cottage, and it hangs in the hall at the manse in Dulwich. It was beautiful weather and we had a lovely time, but there was a hard time ahead.

The Cancer Retreats

Soon the holiday was over - we packed up and left the cottage regretfully. It had been a lovely time. No more chemotherapy with its anti-sick pills and feeling awful. Now it was the machines with the rays.

Over this period we were still planning the pilgrimage/sabbatical, and had been in touch with our friends Ian and Linda who lived at Tolsta Chaolais on the Isle of Lewis. Tim and Rebekah had had a holiday with them - Tim loved it but it was a bit wild and empty for Rebekah. Ian and Linda had been members at my church in Moseley, Birmingham, and had run the Scouts and Cubs between them with great success - Tim being a Scout at the time. Now a parcel arrived in the post from them. It was full of evening primrose oil capsules and with them a letter explaining that Ian felt they might be helpful. Ian works at the Callanish factory, a branch of Scotia Holdings. It had been a fish drying plant, but the firm had gone bankrupt and the drugs firm had picked it up very cheaply. Who wants a factory in the desolate windswept Western Isles? But it was perfect for installing a large distillation and purification plant.

At this point I must explain that Callanish was linking up with several things in our thoughts. I have already said it was mentioned in a book as a start of someone's pilgrimage (I must try to find which book). Both Chris and I had read William Horwood's book 'Callanish'. It is about the escape of a golden eagle from London Zoo, of its journey to Callanish as a place of magical power and its return to bring freedom to other eagles caged there. It is a book about captivity and freedom, the power of freedom over captivity lodged in the stones of Callanish (a complex stone circle not far from the Callanish factory, which is as important as Stonehenge). Not only that, but Chris had found amongst some posters she had a large photograph of some of the Callanish stones. She had kept it from Birmingham days where she was a local Christian Education Movement secretary. It was part of a religious education project on the theme of stones. She had put it up in the cottage kitchen in the hope that we might just get there on the pilgrimage.

Now here was a parcel - and on the plastic containers holding the evening primrose oil capsules was the name 'Callanish' - all just associations, of course, but strange that we'd never come across any of these things before. The association of Callanish with freedom was one we both made - all very pagan, perhaps.

With Ian's note was a photocopy of a paper about research into the radiation of pigskin, which showed considerable evidence that evening primrose oil reduced the burning effect of radiation on it. It could be surmised, then, that it might have the same effect on human skin, and that therefore higher and greater doses of radiation could be given. Added to this, Ian said there was evidence too, that evening primrose oil contained a substance that might be effective as an anti-cancer drug, destroying cancer cells without affecting ordinary cells. It was all very interesting. Ian's boss was a leading pharmacologist and very much believed in this natural drug but other pharmacologists were very sceptical.

For both of us the name linked it with the lovely primroses in the garden at the cottage which we had admired in the spring. It was another of Chris's goals to see them again. I know the evening primrose is not the same plant, but the name is the same.

So Chris began taking three or four capsules a day and we took the research paper to show the doctors at King's College Hospital. There was no official comment except, "If you think they'll do you some good maybe they will - they'll not do any harm". More positive thinking - in line with Chris's attitudes. That was certainly a very important parcel from Ian and Linda. We both had a feeling that somehow we were going to get to Callanish.

Now it was 40 radiotherapy treatments, which is the maximum permitted. It had been the maximum dosage of chemotherapy, but that had failed. If this failed there was nothing that could be done. We were clear about that. One dose per day five days a week was eight weeks, but with the machine having to be serviced occasionally it meant even longer. It was obvious that was the end of any idea of a holiday that summer. What a good thing Chris had insisted on that week after Easter and the week after Tim's wedding. My diary became full of times. 9.30, 9.45, 11.0, 10.30, 10.00, 9.30 - so it went on. First Chris had to go to St Thomas's hospital to be marked up. She said she felt like a piece of meat being dealt with, rather than a person when measured up, drawn on and tattoo marks made. It was all necessary, of course, but very impersonal, and she felt rather degraded. I dropped her off for the first treatment at King's (Thank goodness she didn't have to go all the way to St Thomas's each time). Generally she was treated more or less on time. She had to be held in position very carefully by various bits of equipment and there were guards to stop the rays going elsewhere. She had to keep very still for the whole time of exposure, which was several minutes. No-one else could be with her because of the exposure to the dangerous rays. At least they played music and she used to come home with news of what it was each day. If she moved slightly, it was switched off and they would line her up again. After two treatments the machine broke down and Chris cheered - a day off already. But at lunchtime the telephone rang, "You have been given an appointment at Guy's", she was told. "The consultant says you cannot miss a treatment". On and on it went relentlessly. Wake up, have breakfast, drop Chris off, wait for the 'phone call, drive down, park, and walk into the department to pick her up. It was in a part of King's we'd not seen before. Of course, I was not allowed to see the actual room but Chris made lots of friends - the machine operators and some of the patients. She found it very weakening, and gradually the whole area became quite red.

After about ten treatments, there was an appointment to see the doctor. It was a junior doctor still taking exams. She was cheery and enthusiastic, and we both liked her very much. The measuring was done again. The lump was smaller - already! She obviously hadn't expected it yet - but there it was. I wondered if perhaps she wasn't any good at measuring. It's very difficult to tell the edge of a lump, but she was positive and reassuring. It was working better than expected. We hardly dared to believe it. But after a further ten treatments there was no doubt about it, it was definitely quite a lot smaller. Gradually over the period the area of treatment got less. At first it included her neck where she'd had the operation and also under her arm.

A great hardship to Chris was that the whole area had to be kept as dry as possible, she couldn't wash it. For me it would have been no great disaster but she missed her shower every morning. There was another positive development - her hair was growing again, quite thick and curly. It wasn't fit to be seen yet, but the hairnet or woolly cap were discarded in bed. What a relief! Things were looking up. So far the skin wasn't blistering - good old evening primrose oil doing its stuff.

It was during this period that she read 'Cancer Ward' by Solzenitzen. It was a book she had borrowed from Rebekah. She found it quite fascinating, even though the consultant seemed quite appalled when she told her. It was obviously very important to her, as she read it more than once and made extensive notes. The theme is a moving from prison to hospital, which was as restricting as prison, to a time of freedom.

In these notes are cameos, little pictures in words, of some of her feelings and experiences over these recent months. There is the picture of lying down eagerly under the X-rays, trying to will the tumour cells to believe they were breaking up, a picture of the Crab, cancer, grabbing hold of people with his pincers and not letting go until they are dead; a picture of some people submitting to the cancer and giving up, while others go on fighting to live and be free.

Then there is the hospital treatment degrading people so that they are just patients, not people any more; the long hours on a trolley in the corridor waiting, the loss of personal status, just a body to be treated, and plans for the future torn up; the question as to why doctors should make decisions for you; the loss of control of your life into the hands of the medical profession who know best, the rebellion against this doctors' right to decide, to forbid and to expect compliance with their timetable; what is acceptable behaviour, and what is the right treatment; the comparison of being in a hospital regime, or under doctors orders and of being in prison and the loss of freedom. Chris was at this time writing to a person in prison, and could empathise from her position of being under hospital treatment, as she also could with Terry Waite, whose book she was reading.

Besides this, she found great hope in *'Cancer Ward'*. There is the hope of the destructive cancer that has wrecked life suddenly drying up and dying; the discovery of a different set of values and joys; the unimportance of possessions, social success and money - in comparison with freedom; the wonder of the night sky and close companionship with loved ones.

There is the wonderful hope of going out from the hospital treatment into the springtime of God's creation - the catkins, the blossom, the fresh green leaves, turning deadness into life among the trees. Chris particularly latched on to the picture of Oleg, one of the characters in the book, stepping out from the hospital into the springtime - looking around, taking his time and not rushing, and seeing 'his creation day present to himself' - the apricot tree - the miracle of the newly-born world. In her pilgrimage Chris often referred to her 'apricot tree' - for her the symbol of new life, re-creation, resurrection - God's miracle.

Normal life again?

We had faced Chris's imminent death if the radiotherapy failed. I had been faced with it by Judith, a chaplain at King's. We had had a coffee together and she came out with it, "John, have you thought about the possibility that Chris will die?" It was a hard conversation but one I thank her for initiating. I needed to face it; at the time it seemed the most likely outcome. Partners know that sometime death will separate them - it is part of the marriage service but they don't face it except in a crisis, probably not then. So we had both looked death in the face and it was important we did at this time. If we hadn't maybe we would not have had the determination and faith to go on the pilgrimage. It was all part of the preparation.

After Tim's wedding, we went to our old Liverpool church, Westminster Road, and to visit a lifelong family friend in Wigan in the afternoon. We went to see my aunt in Halifax and a couple of Chris's friends from Camberwell Green who had gone to live in a cottage in Halifax. We went to my other aunt in Wakefield and then went over to Ilkley and visited Helen in the Bradford hospital where she was doing a three month fill-in job. Chris never said as much, but I wondered if she felt she was saying goodbye to the folk in the North.

We also went to the Birmingham church in Moseley on the first weekend after she started the radiotherapy, and maybe she felt that would be a goodbye, too. But some figures at the top of her diary page spell out the good news - 6 x 7 first week; 6 x 5 third week; 5 x 3 fourth week; 4 x 3 fifth week. The measurements of the lump in centimetres. After that it was too diffuse to measure - the radiation had caused too much debris to analyse what it was.

The cottage was a marvellous place to run to when we'd time - usually on Friday after the treatment until Saturday evening. The family news was good. Sue announced she was expecting her second child, and Helen at last got a permanent job in Colchester. At last, on October 12th, came the final radiotherapy session (they started on August 18th) and, of course, we celebrated all three events - any excuse for Chris! The following weekend she celebrated her freedom by going to Uxbridge to see Sue, Simon and Matthew on her own and was at the church when Sue was made a member. Things did begin to get back to normal, but, of course, there were downs. One was on October 3rd when she decided it was right to resign her ministry at Camberwell Green as from the end of November. She'd been putting it off, but realised that even if she made a good recovery she would not be fit to go back before our Sabbatical/ Pilgrimage. It would be June before she could take up work again and it was not fair to keep them hanging on so long. It was a big decision to make. The other one I remember vividly was when the burn marks were healing up and the dead skin flaking away. She sat there in tears and showed me. "Look", she said, "the same old red patch. It hasn't gone. It's just the same. I've had all that treatment and it's done no good at all". I'm afraid she used a few words no minister who has promised to live a holy life should ever use. I didn't know what to say. The hospital were so sure it was much better and they proved to be right. In a day or two the red patch flaked off too. On October 26th Chris attended a lovely event at King's College Hospital. The chapel had been re-decorated, and there was a service for its re-dedication at which Bishop Simon Phipps came, a choir sang and Chris did a prayer. The bishop was very full of 'flu but managed it nevertheless. Chris asked me to take photos of all the clergy - Judith and Stuart (the two Church of England Chaplains), the Bishop, the two catholic clergy, and herself resplendent in her lovely stole. They came out really well and Stuart had one enlarged and framed for Chris. It eventually arrived in May/June time and cheered her up when she was pretty ill.

We had a much deserved holiday - at the cottage, of course, and above that week and the next Chris wrote "still shrinking!" The effects of radiotherapy last for a long time and though they did not rule out an operation, it was put off to see if the lump would shrink right away, which in fact it did. On November 19th 1993 we both went to Sayers Common to the Fairmile Fellowship quiet day. We neither of us sat in the "little wooden house" or wrote any prayers that have been preserved, but we had a walk together and thanked God for returning health, and listened to someone talking about icons.

We came to Advent and Chris went to Camberwell Green on her last Sunday as minister, not to take the service but to take the Advent candles. Two Sundays later she was off to the Russian Orthodox church in London to see one of the King's College Hospital porters, confirmed. He was thrilled that she went. Her wisdom tooth extraction at the Dental Hospital was cancelled and she was able to go to the Hospital Chaplains Christmas lunch instead which delighted her. Two days later, at the Nursery Christmas party, she went without her wig for the first time in public. She threw the wig down the garden to show how she'd hated it - but then retrieved it when the weather-man said it was going to rain!

We had a wonderful family treat at Christmas with almost everyone there watching the Nutcracker ballet at the Royal Festival Hall - it was Dave's idea and it was magic!

With the permission of the hospital we booked for our trip to Rome and Assisi with the 'Magic of Italy'. The Assisi part was left to us to arrange - the other was a package deal which seemed pretty good value, although later we realised it wasn't really in a very convenient part of Rome. We booked for the Fairmile Fellowship and Ministers and Spouses conferences; Iona was not available for Easter unless we stayed nine days, so we booked for just three days two weeks after Easter. The money for the sabbatical had come through generous grants from the URC and Southern Province.

It was, therefore, a happy end to 1993 and a hopeful start to 1994. Chris wrote in her Christmas card and present record book: "We got very tired this year. Even John said he felt his age! But we came through - smiling, we hope! Dave said, 'Now for the survivor's photo!!' Hadn't energy to put new film in!! We had a pretty good excuse! Cancer spoiled 93! - Roll on February 94!".

Our sights were set firmly towards the start of the pilgrimage. It was all working out beautifully and would be a lovely spiritual journey in each other's company. We needed rest, relaxation and inspiration and the cottage and the pilgrimage would give them to us. We would have a wonderful time and the thoughts and prayers of so many people were with us as we looked forward. The cottage would be a place of healing this coming spring, it would be a very special time. And so it was, but not in the way we had planned.

Christmas, New Year, and After

I was in a really funny mood Christmas Day, at least early on. I got up on my own, made the breakfast and felt thoroughly miserable - sitting there on my own eating puffed wheat like any other day. It was so different from the years surrounded by excited children emptying their Christmas stockings. I expect it was really because Christmas day was on a Saturday, and it was followed by the normal Sunday service the next day that I felt very badly done by, neither Helen nor Chris could snap me out of it. But one of my Elders, David, could - acting about with the little children opening their presents in church, their wide-opened eyes as he brought out his enormous present to open, peering in the big box to find the tiny present. I began to laugh, and Christmas had started for me. The next day when I'd said there'd be nobody there after Christmas Eve and Christmas Day, we had a church full, all enjoying drawing round their feet to make their footprints in paper down the aisle. But it caused great amusement, and it was a lovely Christmas after all - with Matthew making everyone laugh with his antics.

It was Chris's turn to be in a funny mood over New Year. When she was supposed to be dancing to pop music and sipping champagne, she was found in the kitchen admitting she'd rather have been in church! What it is to have parents who are both ministers! Dave and Ruth really tried hard and at least we managed some cheers, laughs and songs (?) as the new year dawned. We thought of the Birmingham new year parties with their very Scottish influence - the first footing, the coal, the smoked salmon and the 'wee dram'.

Perhaps Chris felt so guilty about her funny mood that she decided to have a 'Burns' night'. She'd spotted some haggis in the butcher's shop, so on the appointed day our Scottish neighbours, Jim and Mary, and our grass widower, church secretary George (Vera had gone 'home' to Jamaica and left him for a week or two) arrived. I managed to recite 'Some hae meat and canna eat, and some would eat that want it, but we hae meat, and we can eat and so the Lord be thankit'. I'd had ten years practice in Moseley! George tried to look as if he understood. We all tried to demolish two haggises between us, with the 'neeps' and 'tatties', and felt so full we could hardly stand. Chris complained of feeling a little drunk, and we all had a lovely time.

Soon there was good news from Tim. Chris had gone up to Grimsby on her own in November to see him and Rebekah, and they were full of going to Huddersfield to meet the elders of the four churches in a group, and the other minister, whom Chris knew through her training days (Chris always seemed to know people everywhere). Now Tim had been to " preach with a view", the churches had issued a call and he had accepted. We were all really delighted for him. His ordination was set for July 30th, after Tim had finished his course, and the first date the moderator could manage. We'd laughed at Tim in a cassock and dog collar over new year - I think he was wearing a funny hat - now it was really going to happen. Tim was thrilled it was within sight of the Pennines, with snow in winter and the Keighley and Worth valley railway in summer. There was also some lovely news from Helen. We were hearing about a certain pharmacist called Andy! We didn't see him till February, but we gathered he was 'special' and we were very pleased, of course. Christmas and New Year are followed by Helen's birthday which is always special. We gave her the book 'Wild Swans', but she didn't come home for her birthday this time - there were attractions elsewhere! Colchester was proving to be a special place for her!

In the Week of Prayer we had an Agape meal at Dulwich Grove. Chris took the service part really well, and lots of people came to eat in the church sanctuary which the church felt was appropriate.

Chris planned to follow her "Burns' night" with a visit to Birmingham. She'd been looking through her Christian Education Movement things and had dug out a school project on 'stones' and found a lovely poster of the standing stones of Callanish. She put it up at the cottage. In her study she had put up another CEM poster of 'The black Christ'. Now she was going to Birmingham, to the Seva Sadan birthday party, taking the train from London and staying overnight. The previous summer, while at the cottage, we had bought some little Indian bells at the Pestalozzi Village open day, and playing them with the little hammer had brought back memories of her work teaching Asian women English, both in Walsall and Birmingham. It was something she missed in Dulwich and Camberwell, and she was going to see our dear friend, Kumud Christian from Gujerat, who sought to be a friend to the Gujeratis who had settled in Sparkhill. Seva Sadan means 'house of friendship' and the Moseley church had had a strong association with it when we were there. Their Birthday Party was full of Asian culture, and the food and the dancing were very special. But eventually Chris had to admit she didn't feel brilliant. It wasn't just the wine at the Burns' night, maybe it wasn't just a funny mood at New Year. She had had her wisdom tooth out eventually, soon after Christmas, and had been to the hospital for some more tests, though they were negative, thank goodness. She'd gone to a conference on AIDS - was it the subject that made her feel a bit sick? And her old organist at Camberwell, Katie, was really very ill and eventually died. January's a funny month - a long month. Christmas and New Year festivities set you up for a while, but by the end of the month they've worn off. The last straw was a fall at the cottage - off the bottom step onto the grass. As she said, "I saw the primroses and snowdrops from ground level!" I'd said, "Go on, you're imagining it, walk confidently, you'll be all right." I felt differently when I had to pick her up. We imagined it was a 'fluey virus, having heard of several people with similar things, but it was no good, we had to go to the doctor with it, and Seva Sadan was not going to be possible for her.

She wrote to her friends: "It is Sunday evening (at the cottage) - 8 o'clock - and we are just listening to the Classic FM evening concert! John said at about 6.10 'You would just have been arriving at Euston.' I feel very sad to have missed out on my weekend in 'Brum', but it was nice to chat to both you and Kumud and catch up on news. I'm feeling a lot better, but I really couldn't have managed to come. I'm still 'seasick'. We're getting some strong vitamin C tomorrow! (at Battle - she hated taking it!). Hope the family are well! I do hope you didn't go to a lot of trouble before my cancellation. We will try to come again during our sabbatical - or in the summer. Sorry once again to let you all down."

It went very much against the grain - she hated giving in to things. And the worst thing was that the doctor had been in touch with the hospital and they had suggested a head scan. They'd already done a CT scan of her neck, which was negative, and she hated it: "I'm not having one - they can't force me to. It's only a funny virus." But she was on tablets again - 'Stemetil', anti-nausea tablets. When we got back from the cottage we heard that the hospital had been looking for us, there was a vacancy on the CT scan and they were going to fit Chris in, but she'd missed it by being away. We looked at one another - the hospital was after her again - the little bit of freedom was coming to an end. The scan was fixed for Friday, February 4th, the same day as Katie's funeral which I was due to take. The consultant would have the results the same day. We both got sinking feelings in our stomachs. Chris had to keep lying down. I kept hoping she'd say she felt better, but she didn't.

28

A Horrible Day

The preparations were virtually over and arrangements were made. The cottage was ready to receive us - well stocked with clothes, equipment and food, so that we could move in and make it our home without relying on anything from our house in Dulwich. The sabbatical was almost upon us, just ten days away; a service with a baptism coming up in two days for me, a service and presentation for Chris at Camberwell and then a quiet evening communion at Dulwich Grove. The following Sunday was when Revd Lesslie Newbigin was presenting us with shells of pilgrimage, and the whole family would be with us to share in the event and in a family meal to celebrate our pilgrimage starting. Then to Fairmile Court for a quiet retreat for a few days. Italy was booked, Iona was booked, the Ministers conference was booked. It was all systems go from now on. We had made spiritual preparations with prayers, and with reading books - including *Callanish* and *Cancer Ward*, and Gerard Hughes' *In Search of a Way*. Themes were floating in our minds, from the life of St Francis, from *A Christian in Rome*, but there was also the belief that a pilgrimage should be allowed to develop, rather than be too planned. It should be about meeting people on the way, and reacting to circumstances as they presented themselves. Things that happened should be looked at for their spiritual significance - perhaps symbolic things would happen - their symbolism being seen later. Pilgrimage was for living through, a special time walking with God and learning of God. We were to find that what we had been through in the year or so before was to have a great impact on our pilgrimage, indeed to understand its real significance it is completely necessary to know and understand what happened to us beforehand. It is as if at this point we have at least most of the pieces of the jigsaw, and they all fit together, but it needs the pilgrimage to put them together to make the complete wonderful picture. Or it is as if God has in his hands all the strands of wool for the tapestry, and we can see some of these strands in our planning and our living, but only now does He begin to weave the tapestry - to be finished at the end of our pilgrimage. Life is, of course, all a pilgrimage, but for us these next six months were to be very special and meaningful. It was as if our living went up a gear - every moment significant, every day full of meaning, even simple things became important and often symbolic.

We both kept fairly detailed diaries- Chris's longer than mine. It's a good thing we did, for so much happened, often in rapid succession, that it might well have been forgotten. Both of us took photos as well, and they served as aids to memory. We kept souvenirs, and in the house in Dulwich and at the cottage there are pictures and cards full of memories.

One such card remained on our meal table for many months, sent by a friend on Chris' birthday, May 23rd 1993, (though he wasn't aware of it). It contains good wishes for her cancer treatment, and for her to be well enough to be able to take Tim and Rebekah's wedding. The front of the card has a 'Morning Prayer': it says 'Lord, help me to remember that nothing is going to happen to me today that you and I together can't handle'.

On February 4th we read it, I'm sure, as we sat down to breakfast - no doubt at different times, as we almost always did. I can't wait for breakfast, but Chris had to be well washed and showered first. We did not know it was the first day of the pilgrimage, it shouldn't have been in our planning, but God knew, and had prepared us for this day.

Two things were happening at once and it was impossible now to change that unfortunate circumstance, or God's planning? Chris got up and was very wobbly, needing me to hold her up when she walked. It was arranged that our neighbour would come with us to the hospital and remain with Chris while she waited for the scan, and meet her outside afterwards. Then Yvonne from the church would come to the hospital and stay with her to see the consultant and get the results. The scan was at 1 pm, the consultant interview at 2.30 pm - hospital time, of course!

I was taking Katie's funeral at nearby Camberwell Green church - 2 pm at the church, 3 pm at the crematorium.

I put in my diary 'Great trepidation about Chris's head scan - did very little am. Chris falling about, headachey, me preparing for Katie's funeral'. Katie had wanted to die for some while, she was in quite a lot of pain from her back, and bedsores from lying down. She was suffering from breast cancer too and it was a relief when she finally got her wish. I had stayed a while with Chris, parking by the church and walking back to the hospital. She and Jim were sitting facing a blank wall - they said it was like being in the cinema waiting for the film to start! It's strange what thoughts come at these tense times! At the funeral the church was quite full and I was talking to all Chris's congregation, and getting to know some of Katie's relatives. They didn't know the turmoil I was in. My organist, Gillian, was playing the organ and had brought a tape of 'Songs of the Auvergne'. Chris knew Katie had liked them, and suggested playing one of them as the coffin was taken out of the church. Katie had had students from time to time living with her in a flat at the large house, and one of these, now a Baptist minister, spoke at the service. There were a few humorous times remembered - it wasn't too sad, and the song at the end was like Katie herself singing. It was a slow journey to the crematorium through various traffic jams - then the committal, and more talk with relatives and friends.

A minister has to play his part, and can't hurry things on, but I was very agitated as I left, making excuses for Chris and me for not being at the family and friends gathering afterwards. I'm sure they had no idea of the significance of the test and consultant appointment. I got in the car and dashed to the hospital, trying to force myself to slow down and take care. The result of the test would affect our whole future - I was well aware of that. I arrived breathless at the clinic. She wasn't waiting in the waiting room, nor was Yvonne. Perhaps she was having the interview now? I saw the consultant through the open door of her room . She looked up and saw me and she didn't smile and I guessed it was bad news. I walked in to her office, a thing you can't do without invitation. "Is it bad news?" I asked. "I'm afraid so", she said. "Is it a brain tumour?" - I voiced for the first time my fears. "Yes", she said. I felt faint. I sat down in her tiny office. She waited a moment for me to recover a little and then said, "I'm so sorry but please can you sit somewhere else, I'm dealing with another patient." At that moment a nurse came in - we'd met lots of times before - she took me into another room, and I sat down and she brought me a drink. "I'm so sorry", she said. I said, "Chris and I had such plans. Where is she?" "She's just coming out in a minute". And then Chris came out of another room, on Yvonne's arm. She smiled at me and said, "I'm all right". There was no fear in her face - she was in control, and I had gone to pieces. I think the consultant felt I should have been there for the interview. She didn't know I had to take that funeral, it had to be me, deputising for Chris. But she was lovely. She arranged to see us both together, and went through it all again and, of course, all her other patients had to wait. Oh dear - I wonder what they thought of us? Afterwards Chris and Yvonne said I'd gone as white as a sheet. There were secondaries in the brain. The scan showed one but they were fairly sure there were more that didn't show. There was no question of an operation. They had given her an injection of steroids, and she was to take the maximum dose of steroid tablets each day, and would be given a course of radiotherapy to her head - she would lose her hair again. The treatment was palliative only - it was incurable. She had terminal cancer.

I was bewildered. Yvonne had gone to the pharmacy to get all the tablets. I confessed I'd already mixed some up that morning - gave her Tamoxifen instead of Stemetil, which just aggravated her giddiness. Now it was Stemetil, Dexamethasone, Tamoxifen, blood pressure tablet, Evening Primrose Oil, and yet more tablets to stop the Dexamethasone upsetting her stomach. She was in a wheelchair now and had to be taken to the loo by a nurse, and I was wandering around not knowing what to do. Good old Yvonne came back and took charge of me. "Go and get the car, and I'll be outside with Chris in the wheelchair, and I'll come back with you if you like." Eventually we got home and Yvonne cooked a meal for us, and refused payment for the drugs from the pharmacy. Only when I had collected myself a bit did I realise I'd got my suit and clerical collar on. I'd made such a commotion and exhibition of myself, and everyone had been ministering to me. But we did manage to eat some tea. Then there were the phone calls to make to all the family and more tears. We determined that everyone must know at the church - it must not be hidden. Dear George, my church secretary, came and said prayers with us. He was so lovely that evening, and we got a bit of sleep that night, in spite of everything.

The following day I steeled myself to go to the coffee morning at church and face them all, knowing at least they all knew the situation. Everyone was so kind to me and we were all upset and emotional together. For the next day or so I was not too bad when I was with Chris, but when I was away from her I just felt I wanted to cry, though actually I didn't. And I felt Chris drifted away from me. I couldn't understand how she could be so calm and bright, and able to smile as if nothing was wrong.

I was in turmoil - I was going to lose her. I remembered seeing a good friend in the last stages of a brain tumour. Would it be like that? Chris had been given lots of pain killers along with all the other drugs - would her death be really painful? I wondered how I was going to cope with services on Sunday, of how or if Chris would get to her presentation, and I thought of all our plans for the pilgrimage, all shattered to bits. Would we even be able to get to the cottage? Was there any point in a 'send-off' service, with our shells being presented - could Chris even get to the service? And what about Sue and Simon coming on this Sunday with Matthew, and us supposed to be looking after Matthew on the Monday for Sue and Simon to go out for the afternoon and evening together?

I couldn't see then that the pilgrimage had started, that we were living it, and that Chris was looking death straight in the face with no fear, destroying its power. She was as serene as I was in turmoil. Her brain was working overtime, making decisions for me, showing me what to do. She took charge from this moment on - the pilgrimage was happening, and it had a new dimension. It was to be a pilgrimage to death, and she was not afraid. Nothing was going to stop her **living.** But she had looked death in the face once before, in the summer, and that had been a vital part of her preparation for her spiritual journey. The weaver was beginning to weave. The bits of jigsaw would begin to fit together now. All had been a preparation. Now we were starting out together on a journey of a lifetime, except we weren't together. I couldn't understand her, and she couldn't explain. I had to face her impending death in my own way, she couldn't help me, though she worried about me and prayed for me. She had the cancer - I should have been helping her, but she was helping me.

It is, I think, quite significant that I took a funeral service that day, seeking to come to terms with death in a spiritual way for the family concerned, yet when faced with it in my own married life I couldn't cope - but Chris could. Perhaps it was as well I was not at the first interview with the consultant. Perhaps Chris could not have coped if I had been with her, going to pieces.

For me, one of the themes of the pilgrimage was a coming to term with the impending death of the one who was most important to me, whom I loved the most, with whom I shared everything. And Chris's attitude to it had a great impact on me. We were not going on separate spiritual journeys, our pilgrimage was together, and we supported and challenged one another along the way.

PART II
THE PILGRIMAGE

The Week Before the Send-off

On the Saturday Chris was feeling a bit better, so we decided to tell Camberwell Green she would be at the service, all being well. Sunday morning was a scramble to get ready, bringing back memories of happier times when it was normal for us to go to our respective churches. We got to Camberwell Green, and I helped her up the steps and into the church, it was difficult for her physically, but her smile was broad as she met her congregation after so long. We did not know then, but it was to be her last visit. Then I was off to Dulwich Grove. It was as well I had prepared fully before the Friday, and all was arranged before we had the news. Ruth Clarke was there - specially visiting to meet with Prince Aryee, the father of the baby to be baptised that day, who comes from Big Ada in Ghana with which Dulwich Grove has a special relationship (I remember Prince was waiting in the out-patients with me when I was waiting for Chris after the original biopsy when she was told she had cancer, nearly a year before). Ruth and her husband, Raymond, were just about to visit Ghana, and would be visiting Big Ada. I told Ruth the news. She was very shocked and gave me a big hug. I felt very emotional. Gradually it was getting around the church. I was able to tell the congregation that our pilgrimage would not be as planned and my voice stayed firm. It was lovely to have the baptism, and the photos afterwards and I found I could smile quite naturally. I preached about the importance of everyone, how I had never baptised my own children - I needed someone else to do that, how prayers with me in the vestry were important, and how we should support each other. How true I have found that since - a minister in trouble needs such a lot of support, and Dulwich Grove has helped so much.

Then I was off to Camberwell Green to pick up Chris - she was radiant. They'd had a special choir, and all had gone well. As usual she talked and talked, but was pretty tired. She saw her name up in gold letters with the other ministers, and she had received a communion set, but didn't open it till she got home. She was given flowers, too. We got back very late, but it didn't matter.

In the afternoon Sue, Simon and Matthew arrived and the stress and tension disappeared. I went off to take the evening service with a heavy heart. It was communion and I wanted to share it with Chris, but she was not fit. I was having to learn that her illness was coming between us in our worship. The theme was Candlemas, and I used some poems from the Iona Coracle, and a very set communion; I could not trust myself to do anything that wasn't written down. I felt very lonely without her in the congregation and again felt we were drifting apart.

In the evening we put on some very old colour slides, and we all enjoyed looking at them. It was good to look back, and take our minds off the present and the future.

The next day Simon and I went for a long walk. I have found walking a great therapy, a time to get rid of pent up emotion in hard exercise. Walks on my own have helped me to cope with the reality of the cancer, but it was good to talk to Simon, and to see the first signs of spring blossom, snowdrops, and brightly coloured ducks in their spring plumage. Then our GP arrived. Chris and I were together for the interview, which pulled no punches. She was gentle, but quite straight with us and at the end we knew where we were. Chris was going to die; we could not go to Italy. The doctor would sign forms for us to reclaim the money from the insurance. She was very supportive and said when we needed her she would do all she could to help. I suggested Chris might be able to go to the cottage and have the radiotherapy to her head at Hastings and she said she'd ask our consultant. But soon after she'd gone the phone rang and it was St Thomas's hospital. The first of 6 radiotherapy treatments would be there on Thursday - the last one being the following Thursday. The consultant was in charge, not me - and that was that. We couldn't go to Fairmile Court either. This pilgrimage had a life of its own - and neither Chris nor I seemed to be able to control it.

Yet Chris was as bright as a button, talking nineteen to the dozen, so full of life and lots of smiles. The pastoral assistant at Crossway church arrived while I was on the walk, and was so horrified she wrote me a letter of sympathy about having a partner so 'brittle bright' when all you want to do is cry, and she got her husband to come on his motor bike to post it through the door that day. It was very helpful - at least someone understood how I felt.

Then Chris was saying to Sue and Simon, "of course we'll be all right with Matthew, you go off and enjoy yourselves". This had been the plan, long before, that they would go out to a meal and the theatre and leave Matthew with us. Chris was adamant. How we coped I don't know. I made the meal and went to the shops and gave him his bath. Chris taught him 'I love the sun' and did painting with him. She was making the most of the little time she had left with her grandchild, saying prayers with him, playing games, entering into his childhood.

At last he was happily asleep and suddenly she had time for me, and the gap between us disappeared as physically, emotionally and spiritually we came as close as we could. It was to be the last time we made love - the radiotherapy seemed to change her in that regard. But it didn't matter. From this time on until her death we remained very close emotionally and spiritually, and although our minds took us along different paths, that did not divide us, but made our relationship more creative. Suddenly I was able to smile and laugh with her - we were going to live. From that time we seemed to live on a higher plane than normal, as if she was already glimpsing heaven and taking me with her.

The following day was back to some kind of normality, however. Our neighbour had had a fall, and messed up his face. I contacted the insurance people about cancelling the holiday, and Lesslie Newbigin about the Sunday morning service; thankfully David had offered to do the evening for me. Lesslie would preach and present our shells of pilgrimage. The idea of the shells came partly from the badge which is used by Churches Together in England, and partly from the Horniman exhibition about pilgrimage to St James at Santiago de Compostella. The pilgrims wore scallop shells; no one knows the origin of the custom, but it goes back to the 12th century when the shells seem to have been deliberately adopted as a badge in imitation of the Jerusalem pilgrim who wore a cross blessed by the church, and came back with a palm. It may have started with an enterprising market trader selling them and telling the pilgrim they came from the sea like St James. Before that I suppose the scallops were eaten and the shells thrown away. So we wanted our shells and ourselves to be blessed at our send-off session. The shells had been donated by Mabel, my stepmother, who gave them to us when we first mentioned the idea.

There was a meeting with George about the next week's elders' meeting, the final talk before we went away. I would not be at the meeting, of course, and in the evening there was the final interview with three people coming into membership on Sunday; typically for Dulwich Grove, a South Londoner born and bred, a Jamaican, and a Ghanaian. They each chose a hymn for the service, and all were very concerned about Chris and me and how we were coping.

It was around this time that Chris got the Christmas book out; her record of Christmas cards and gifts each year, and prepared it for me for the next Christmas without her. She did it when I was out, so I didn't find it till Christmas 1994, but she did tell me she'd been writing out for me, 'how to do Christmas'. She stuck in a little poem, cut out from somewhere:-

'Old messages and new friends
Familiar texts and fresh meanings
Customary feasts <u>but never the same people</u> (her underlining)
That is Christmas'.

She wrote detailed instructions as to where things were: the Christmas table cloth and serviettes, the crackers and Christmas cards we'd bought in the January sales, the address books. She told me to write a Christmas letter as she always did and duplicate it as usual, to put up the Advent calendar and light the Advent candle. She explained how to thaw the turkey, and not to forget to change the beds and the towels for the visitors, and to invite Dave and Ruth to put up the Christmas tree and do the decorations. She even suggested some presents to buy for people. It was entitled 'How to do Christmas 94 - or 95? - or 96?'.

On the Wednesday we went off to the hospital to see the consultant again. I dropped Chris off as parking near seemed impossible, and she seemed much steadier, but she wobbled between the parked cars, nearly fell, and grabbed hold of a lamp-post. I, kicking myself for dropping her off like that, sat there helpless in a line of cars waiting for the traffic lights. But God was looking after us - all those prayers from people! - and along came a kind lady who took Chris's arm and led her off into the hospital, where it turned out she worked at the WRVS tea-bar! I parked at a church member's flat and soon Chris and I were together in the clinic waiting room, and she was having a long talk with a Judge's wife who was a bit deaf, so everyone in the room shared the conversation! The consultant talked about the future - everything seemed more hopeful. She told me in detail how to scale down the steroids as the radiotherapy took effect. She thought our journeying might well be possible, including Iona and the Hebrides, though we would have to wait and see, and of course Italy and Fairmile Court were already cancelled. I think she was pleased how Chris looked now the steroids were taking effect, though she was still on the maximum dose. In the afternoon the Moderator, David Helyar, arrived, everyone was so concerned for us. He was very helpful, and when I said I wondered if I ought to return some of the Sabbatical money as we were not going to Italy after all, he told us, "Keep it - spend it how you like. Everyone concerned would want you to have it for yourselves, knowing what has happened". And I'm sure we did spend it on ourselves during our very special time. Chris joked that a lot of it was going on her drugs - not really, but they were quite an item.

On the Thursday I went to the early morning clergy prayers for the last time till nearly the end of May, at St John's - about the saints Benedict and Scholastica. It was a cheerful breakfast, and I felt the support of everyone for us. They too, were very shocked by the news and wanted to help all they could. St Thomas's had offered hospital transport for us, and we'd accepted because car parking was pretty awful, if not impossible there, and very expensive. It came very early with the result that we had a two hour wait, but eventually she went in. The first treatment took a long time as they had to line everything up and arrange shields. They explained the rays would go in by her eyes, and so there were lead shields for them. We just hoped they knew what they were doing. The machine seemed to be on a long time, and if she moved it all had to be stopped and lined up again. Gloria from the Copleston Centre Church worked there, and she was a lovely friendly face bearing cups of tea for us and having time to chat. She was literally God-sent, I'm sure. The registrar came to talk to me while Chris was having the treatment, and told me cheerfully of someone who had had this treatment two years ago and was still fine.

We had a really long wait for the car back, but Chris was occupied in mental imaging again, as in the book '*Getting Well Again*'. The first radiotherapy machine was the washing machine, getting out all the dirty cancer cells. Then the one that came really close was Brian the Snail from the Magic Roundabout. The CT scan was Terry Waite's fridge where he had nearly suffocated. What about this one? Oh yes, of course. Mr McHenry's hat! Is that from the

Magic Roundabout too? Neither of us were sure, but the mental image was a comic one, suiting her mood of excitement and cheerfulness. Was it the steroids or a spiritual state coming from being uplifted by all the prayers? She certainly remained radiant - really alive with the joy of living - and talking to everyone.

On Friday we were visited by Judith - Chris's colleague at King's chaplaincy. We talked about the family and she looked at the photos of their weddings, and of Helen with her Romanian children. We showed her the big photo of the cottage that my brother had taken in the summer. She talked about how Chris had helped her in previous months and how she was looking forward to her ordination on Pentecost eve at Southwark Cathedral. We said it would be lovely to be there with her that day, and she said she'd try to arrange it for us. When we told her we'd be going to the cottage the next Friday, she offered to take communion with us that morning. We were thrilled. Little did we know then, but both she and Lesslie were not only going to send us off on our pilgrimage, but be there at its end when Chris died. And that, I am sure, was God's planning, not ours.

On Friday, too, a very significant thing happened that I was not aware of at the time. Our neighbours, Mary and Jim, had been to a requiem mass for Father Hugh O'Neill, monk and priest at Worth Abbey. We knew him as he often visited St Peter's just down the road, and came to various ecumenical services and events in Dulwich. They gave Chris the order of service. Chris had been reading *Getting Well Again* and in it the author writes, "With time we recognised that since patients could direct the course of their recovery, we also had to admit that they could - and should - direct the course of their dying, if that was the direction in which they wished to move. Now, as part of our programme, we seek to help patients confront their fears and beliefs about death. A square look at the possibility relieves patients of a great deal of anxiety and seems to reduce the physical pain of dying - in fact it is now rare for our patients to suffer a lingering or painful death. We point out to our patients whether or not they recover from the cancer - they have succeeded in improving the quality of their living - or the quality of their dying - and have exercised great strength and courage". Then there are instructions about mental imaging your death and funeral. I cannot be sure, but I am myself convinced that reading this inspired Chris to pick up the order of service for Father Hugh's requiem mass and use it as a basis for her own funeral, which I think she wrote on the Saturday while I was out seeing Lesslie and taking the shells, and then seeing Beti, a church member, also suffering from breast cancer and having chemotherapy and radiotherapy, who was to die soon after Chris. She (Chris) used the gathering song *Kindle a Flame*, all three of the hymns *Praise to the Holiest*, *The Lord's my Shepherd* and *All my hope in God is founded;* two of the three readings *Isaiah 25: 6-9* and *Luke 12: 35-40*, and added excerpts from the booklet *Together in Prayer* that had just arrived for the Womens' World Day of Prayer on March 5th. She included Simon playing *The Swan,* and *The Hebridean Overture'* on tape, and David Helyer to do the address. I'm sure she visualised it all, as she hoped it would happen. Even the readers were named.

When I came back that Saturday for a late lunch she smiled at me and said, "I've been writing my funeral". I couldn't take it. I haven't even mentioned it in my diary - I just had to distance myself from it. I said, "Please Chris, if you must, you must, but put it in the drawer where I know where it is, but can't see it. I can't cope with that". And she understood, and didn't try to force me to see it, not till very much later, after our sabbatical was over.

In her diary, too, she set goals for herself, as it suggests in *Getting Well Again.* On several occasions she said, "I can't seem to get myself into July". But she put down as goals the women's ordinations at Southwark Cathedral, Sue's baby's birth and Tim's ordination. She had difficulty with the last one, but said later "Now I can see myself there". In her diary too, she put against certain events "Please God", and when she came to them "Thank you God". It was all a part of mental imaging which I am sure contributed to her great serenity and cheerfulness which remained with her till her death. It fitted her particular faith and spirituality. It was this week especially where she dealt with herself - got herself sorted out. After this she said about the book *Getting Well Again*, "I've finished with that now". And when she wrote her diary during the pilgrimage, her illness is hardly mentioned. She is living and meeting people, seeing places and enjoying God's world. Her illness and death are accepted and forgotten.

Her thinking and sorting out was all done (just) before all the family began to descend on us that weekend, as instructed. She didn't often instruct the family, but this time they knew they had to be there. 'Mum has issued the edict. We have to come'. Tim is not fond of big family gatherings, but even he knew there was no ducking out of this one. It was the last time we would all be together.

The Send-off and the First House Communion

Tim, Rebekah and Helen had gone for lunch to Mill Hill, to see my Dad and Mabel, on the Saturday. Tim and Rebekah went into central London for an evening out, and Helen came over to Dulwich. When she 'phoned she was at Herne Hill, so I went to pick her up. She was very apprehensive about seeing her Mum, but I reassured her that she was feeling better. After a talkative afternoon, we had a light tea, and prepared to go to the church Valentine's party. It was a sort of send-off before the send-off! A lot of people came and we had a lovely time. We were all supposed to wear something red and Chris had an artificial red rose, with a golden heart, sold for AIDS Day at the hospital, I think. It was a cold night, but the infra-red heaters cast a lovely red glow and everyone was warm - it went really well. Helen felt at home with her Dulwich Grove friends and there was dancing and eats. One member, Olive, fell heavily in a dance and was obviously badly hurt. An ambulance had to be sent for - such a shame - but it was a lovely party even so. At the end I took Chris and Helen back home, to find Tim and Rebekah there, after their evening out. I went off down to the hospital to see how Olive was - it was a long wait for her in casualty - it always is at King's. It was the early hours of the morning before she got a bed - her hip was broken. When I eventually got home, Chris and Rebekah were in bed, and Tim and Helen were enjoying being together - and doing the vegetables and the soup for the special meal the next day. It was a special time for the three of us - coming to terms with the occasion. Family reunions are all very well but you don't have much time for real talking - a lot of it tends to be trivialities.

Chris put at the front of her pilgrimage diary the pilgrimage poem - by Sir Walter Raleigh:

'Give me my Scallop shell of quiet
my staff of faith to walk upon
My scrip of joy, Immortal diet
my bottle of salvation
My gowne of Glory, hope's true gage
And thus I'll take my pilgrimage!'

The shells were all arranged, Chris refused to contemplate a walking stick, the communion for the immortal diet was part of the service, and we would take our scripts - our bibles, our books and prayers, and Chris had ordered her gown of glory from a catalogue. It was to be a primrose dress, to match the primroses at the cottage, but it hadn't come. She had to use another dress, it was a special one nevertheless, to suit the poem. Soon after breakfast, with Rebekah taking the cereal packets for teaching practice(!), the rest of the family arrived, and it was the opportunity to give Helen her presents for her birthday, a fortnight late, but better late than never. Sue gave her Mum a heart-shaped box of chocolates for Valentine's Day. Outside a little snow fell, but nothing significant enough to put people off coming to the service.

Lots of people came. I wore my special stole for the occasion, and Lesslie preached. For the opening of the service I used quotes from St Augustine and St Columba. There's a good connection with St Columba and Iona, but the St Augustine, first Archbishop of Canterbury was another man from the St Augustine, of course - though I still made the connection in my mind!

'Lord, you are great, and greatly to be praised
Awaken us to delight in your praises
for you made us for yourself and our hearts are restless
till they find their rest in you'.

'Be thou a bright flame before me,
be thou a guiding star above me,
be thou a smooth path below me,
be thou a kindly shepherd behind me
today, tonight, and for ever'.

The reading from *Numbers 9* was about the Israelites' pilgrimage in the wilderness, moving only when the pillar of cloud told them to. Chris referred to this in her diary on several occasions as we went from place to place. The reading from *Hebrews 11:1-6* mentions Abraham's faith in God leaving his own country, without knowing where he was going. I spoke to the children about pancake day and the beginning of Lent, and about the pilgrimage poem. Lesslie spoke about moving on when God tells us to, and about how we grow up by losing things, making decisions at various stages in our lives, and therefore losing the opportunity to do other things that we might have done, and how we move on to various stages in our lives, leaving things in the past. Then after I had received the new members, Lesslie gave us our shells. In each he had written *Psalm 121: v8* 'He will protect you as you come and go, now and for ever'. Chris was able to come forward to receive it and Tim took a photo of what was a very special moment. Then there was the communion. It was special to lead it with all the family there. We were presented with a lovely red miniature rose from the church, which still flourishes at the cottage, and my organist gave us a card of two other famous travellers - the Owl and the Pussy-cat! The Vicar and Curate from the Copleston Centre, Cecil and Dianna, came after their service had finished.

Then we had the family celebration meal, and lit two significant candles: Edward's (Chris's organist) peace candle, and one bought at Kevelaer in Germany, a place of pilgrimage with a particularly beautiful shrine that we had visited some years before during our visit to Ina, our German daughter!

It all went very quickly, and very soon people began to leave. Everyone helped with the clearing up, and Tigger, our cat, went with Sue, Simon and Matthew in the cat basket on his holidays with them!

When we were on our own, the phone rang. It was a Presbyterian minister friend from Portland, Oregon. He was involved in our previous sabbatical in 1985 when we had stayed in Oregon for three months. He did not know Chris was so ill and I think he was on the phone nearly half an hour. It was so lovely and so unexpected to hear from him. We had had a telegram from Oregon the day Chris was ordained. Then came a 'phone call from Birmingham wishing us well - so many people shared in our send-off. I wrote in my diary that day 'This day really lived up to all our expectations. We had looked forward to it for such a long time, and it was really happy, just a perfect day. As I relinquished my responsibilities, it seems hard to believe that it will be for three months. I wonder where our journey will lead us, and who we shall meet?'

The next couple of days it snowed. On the Monday it was like a skating rink and all the traffic seemed to be at a standstill. What a good job it hadn't been the day before. We slithered our way to St Thomas's both days. We had found that the best way was for me to join the queue for the car park whilst Chris would get out and walk into the clinic. By the time I'd parked (sometimes it took nearly an hour) she'd be nearly ready to come back having had her treatment. She took her Valentine chocolates down to share with the nurses and with Gloria, who invariably gave us tea and chatted.

Tuesday was Shrove Tuesday and I made pancakes. On Ash Wednesday Chris thought back to her Fairmile retreat the year before which involved 'ashing' and the affirmation of baptism. It was around this time that she used holy water from Walsingham, to put on her forehead each morning which had been given to her by Stuart, the senior chaplain at King's College Hospital.

On the Thursday, I went to collect some gifts from an African lady from Sierra Leone. She thought a great deal of Chris who had read to her from the bible when she was in hospital. There was a necklace with a cross, an African bookmark that Chris used all though the pilgrimage, and a St Christopher badge - the saint for travellers. Eventually Chris took the badge into St Christopher's Hospice with her as she travelled across the river of death. The legend of the saint is important to the hospice, and his carrying the child across the river is the hospice logo. It was the day of the last of the treatments for Chris - a larger one - done in a different way.

At last we were free to go to the cottage and we were all packed up and ready. Chris woke at 4 am remembering more things to pack. Before we went Judith arrived, along with Joyce, chaplain at King's, to take the communion. It was the first time Chris's communion set was used. Chris set out the table with a chalice, her stole and mine, an Iona cross in lace she had made, flowers, and of course, the shells. Judith did it beautifully, and mentioned all the family in the prayers. Though she was not ordained, and did not use the prayer of consecration it made no difference in our free church minds. It was just as valid when she did it for us three months later after her ordination, at the end of the sabbatical. This was to be the first of several home communions.

The Cottage at Last

After Judith had gone, we set off with all our stuff. It was February 18th, only three days after we had planned to leave. We ate sandwiches on the journey. It was a bright sunny day. We had cut the orchid flower off our cymbidium, and cut some daffodil buds from the garden. We took the poinsettia that was still lovely from Christmas, a chrysanthemum plant given by our neighbours, and the miniature rose from the church. The journey took about one and a quarter hours as usual, and we unloaded and went down to the garden centre to pick up some coal and have a cup of tea. I took a photo of Chris by a picture of sunflowers, she looked a bit pale and unwell. She bought a little bird-feeder to hang on a tree.

I put in my diary 'Sun shone till nearly 5 pm. Blackbirds singing, saw chaffinches, wagtail, robin, thrushes. There are primroses, snowdrops large and small, and winter aconite'. I cooked the tea, and we ate the strawberries Judith had brought for us. We had a coal and log fire in the evening.

The charm of our cottage is difficult to describe. The main room and the kitchen face pretty well due South, with the result that in Winter the sun begins to come in at breakfast time, and remains all day. The cottage is on slightly rising ground, so the south side with the entrance is high up, with steps to a porchway with lots of glass. The room is therefore very light, with a view over the garden, and beyond to distant low hills where the Pestalozzi Village is. It is not overlooked by anyone, even in the winter with the leaves off the trees, for it does not face the road. Indeed, it is very difficult to see the cottage from anywhere, even though it is very near the middle of the village. People have walked past the gate without seeing it, yet it is just opposite the village hall, and Roselands, the sheltered housing scheme, and next door to the large Brickwall hotel whose roofs and old fashioned chimneys can be seen through the trees, and on the other side next door to a TV repair place. All around are hedges, fences and trees. The walls of the cottage are thin, so sounds penetrate easily. There is the traffic from the road, which is more comforting than disturbing and you don't feel isolated and lonely. There is the bird-song from the numerous birds in all the trees around. Somehow you feel as if you are nearly outside. When it rains you hear it pattering on the porch roof, and wonder when it will all start dripping into the house, but the roof is good and the cottage is dry. When the wind blows, the rambler rose scrapes against the porch window and the wooden walls now and then, but the windows are tight fitting and it is not in the least draughty.

But the place still has temperature extremes, although I had spent a long time lagging the roof space, having to worm my way into very little spaces to do it, and frightening Chris that I would fall through the ceiling! It heats up quickly, but cools down equally fast! So in the long nights of winter, in spite of 2 storage heaters, the temperature can drop from nearly 70^0 in the evening to 50^0 overnight, and even lower in the bedrooms which are on the North side. The bathroom can be pretty near freezing so a trip to the bathroom at 4 am is quite an experience! It brings back memories of the days before central heating! But with electric blankets, room heaters, and a bathroom infra-red heater, it is quite bearable, and seeing the morning sun coming in at breakfast and when a welcoming fire is lit, it is soon very cosy, and the bills are actually surprisingly low.

The furniture all comes from the previous owner, so is old but comfortable, and adds to the charm of the place. Chris chose the curtains and carpets, which match beautifully. An old couch is covered by an Indian bedspread brought back by one of the boys from South India. A little mat is from Romania. There is no television, but a reasonable quality radio and tape recorder and we listened to lots of tapes and classic FM, and a few radio plays. And there is a telephone but only the family and friends know the number! Chris had many a long phone call. Our neighbours round the other side from the road have the keys, but have never interfered with us and were very helpful whenever we wanted anything.

When Chris first saw it she said, "This is a healing place. I shall get better here". It is quite idyllic and whenever I come I feel stress and worry lifted off me. This time, too, Chris was getting better, but she was still very high on steroids, and the radiotherapy to her head must have had effects on her too, so those first few nights she didn't sleep much. On several nights I heard her pottering around in the kitchen at 2 am Fortunately we had a bedroom each. I couldn't sleep on the double bed we'd bought, I found it too hard, though no-one else has a problem with it. Sometimes I would get up to see what she was doing. She was as bright as a button, as if it was the middle of the day. "I've had a brilliant night", she said. "I've had a wonderful sleep". I left her to get back to bed with the light on and a book to read, with her heater going and a cardigan and gloves on! She described how she saw the dawn coming up, heard the birds on the roof and saw the frost (or sometimes snow) on the big conifer down the garden, and the red berries on the holly illuminated by the rising sun. She was very happy to be free to do just what she liked, with a radio beside her bed if she wanted it. To keep her in bed a little longer I used to get in beside her at around 7 a.m., when I normally woke, and we'd stay there till we'd listened to Thought for the Day, and the weather and news. She missed it if I overslept and then got straight up.

At the beginning of her diary, written just before we got to the cottage, she was looking at some Advent readings.
'O come, 0 come Emmanuel, and ransom captive Israel,
that mourns in lonely exile here, until the Son of God appear. Rejoice, rejoice'
'Remember your word to your servant by which you gave me Hope. This is my comfort in sorrow that your promise gives me life'
'I remember your decrees of old, and these, Lord, console me. I think of your name in the night-time, and I keep your law. This has been my blessing'
'May our world be flooded with the grace of your coming - let us experience the fullness of your joy!'
'May we live our lives to the full in this world - and transfigure it with the hope of future glory!'
'In the tender compassion of our God the dawn from on high shall break upon us, to shine on those who dwell in darkness and the shadow of death, and to guide our feet into the Way of Peace'

Then she writes: "I've been watching a lot of dawns coming up over the past week! It really is the darkest just before the dawn - then it lightens and all the birds (of paradise?) start singing their little hearts out! Sometimes it rains, and it's as if they turn over in the nest and go back to sleep".

And then: "I've been very 'hyper' on my drugs. I had mosaics and frescoes of Italy behind my eyes the first night - the disappointment, I suppose! Then I saw a great coal tip! was it Doncaster where we started our ministry in 1960? Then I saw the surgeon in bed - instead of Dad! Weird! I don't even fancy him at all!"

Beside her bed at the cottage was a book of meditations I had picked up at the Lutheran church in Oberammergau in 1990 when we went with the church. It was of the events leading up to the crucifixion, and meant a lot to her, as she put it specially on one of her 'set up' photos. At the beginning of her diary she pasted these excerpts she had cut from somewhere -

'Pressure ...
Life in the world today is full of pressure and haste. Everywhere you hear the cry "If only I had more time". Even those without employment sometimes wonder how they ever had time to fit in a job as well. This is equally true within the Church. As we rush around swamped by our "busyness" or paralysed by our anxiety, it is all too easy for us to lose our real contact with our God and for our spiritual vision to grow dim'

'Peace
The use of silence in our spiritual life and worship offers us an opportunity to wait upon God and let our spiritual vision be recreated'.

We were indeed fortunate that God had provided for us our wooden house of retreat - our little bit of paradise. We felt free at last, as Oleg did in *'Cancer Ward'*. It was the morning of creation. The world had been created anew for us too. It was the first days of our new lives in pilgrimage. Chris kept talking about Oleg's apricot tree, and looked around in wonder at the signs of spring in the garden.

Visitors and Neighbours

It wasn't a totally new world for us - for we had spent time at the cottage before. The lady across the road used to come in and dust and look after the place for Vera, but she was elderly and had had a fall, and was no longer able to do it. I felt it was right to go over and chat with her about Chris. She was upset, but glad I'd told her, and she kept asking. I've already mentioned our neighbours and at first they hoped for a miracle, but eventually had to accept things as we had. We were on good term with Bill, the gardener at the Brickwall Hotel. He'd been round for a coffee on one occasion. When I told him, he found it very difficult to deal with. "Does she know?" he asked. "Yes, of course!" "How does she deal with it?" he wondered. "How can she cope with knowing?". I told him she was quite able to, and when he saw her he really didn't know what to say. How could she be smiling and behaving normally? We often had a little talk, and he was very helpful to me. I parked the car near his shed, and if he saw me he always wanted to know how things were going. We had been told to register at the local doctor's surgery, which was only the other side of the hotel - very handy. They were very helpful and sympathetic too, and one of the receptionists lived only two doors away, so she often waved to us and was interested to know how we were getting on. They got to know us at the post-office too - everyone was very friendly. I expect it got all round as things do in villages. It was amazing that our two nearest neighbours both had strong connections with Dulwich. One had worked in Dulwich Hospital, and the other had been to school there. I got to know the people in the bank at Battle, and we both were well known in the coffee shop/restaurant there.

One of my church members (she's transferred now) lives up the road at Staple Cross with her sister. They are good friends too, trusted with the phone number! So four days after we arrived, one snowy morning, they rang up to ask if they could call. I'd been out taking photos, and was warming up in the bath when they rang! They called, bearing primulas from the garden centre, and we had a lovely talk, showed them photos and arranged that they would come and share a house communion with us and the pastors of the local Sedlescombe URC, whom we knew. They lived at the other end of Sedlescombe, over the other side of the river Brede.

A few days later the vicar at the Copleston Centre, in Peckham, came to call. His wife, Janet, has family in Hastings, so he thought he'd look for us in a spare half hour. He was lucky to find us - I was walking along the road from parking the car when he saw me - he didn't even know the name of the cottage. Soon after, the same day, a very old friend of mine from my teenage years came for lunch - bearing more primulas.

The next day the organist from Sedlescombe URC called to see us, and our neighbours dropped off two bags of logs for our fire - no charge - their son is a farmer and it's wood off their land. We certainly weren't going to be lonely.

Then Helen came with her friend, Andy, whom we'd never seen. We were dying to know what he looked like. Chris had her camera out, totally embarrassing them both! Oh well - we didn't frighten him off totally! We were just so excited.

There was a visit from one of Chris's very old friends who lives in Worthing. They hadn't seen each other for years, and there was a lot to talk about.

On the 4th March, just a month after the horrible day, we had the house communion. It was the Womens' World Day of Prayer, and we remembered the services going on in the Hastings area and in Dulwich. We sang hymns, including 'Jesus the Lord says' and Chris got up and played the 'temple bells' we had brought from Pestalozzi that reminded us of Birmingham's Seva Sadan and Kumud. It was a lovely service, very informal, and the singing was good. Chris commented in her diary about the prayer that mentions about us all being one in heaven and earth. Ever since Chris's death I have remembered it, and feel especially close to Chris at that time.

A week later we had another communion. Some very old friends, a couple we had known in Walsall 20 years before, came from Chichester and after lunch he led the service. He is a non-stipendiary minister in the Church of England, and resident doctor for the St Wilfrid's hospice in Chichester. So it was very special for us, very thoughtful, based on Habakkuk.

No, we certainly didn't spend our time in lonely isolation on a silent retreat! We went off to Hastings and Bexhill to the theatre and to concerts too. I think we were the only two adults at *'Wind in the Willows'* without children, but we didn't care. Sometimes in the evening we had the projector out, looking at old slides: Ireland, Oberammergau, the Isle of Wight, and Iona.

Somehow it all just happened. We had nothing at all planned for this period when we left home. After all, we should have been to Italy, Rome and Assisi, during this time, and somehow we neither of us minded not going; we both felt perhaps it was just as well. It would have been so busy and stressed. God had other plans and we enjoyed them. And all this time Chris's health was improving. The steroid dosage was going down and down, and apart from one little tumble there'd been no problems.

Finding the Way

From the last chapter it may sound as if we were busy all the time, but of course that was not the case. There was a lot of time when we were on our own at the cottage, enjoying the seclusion and lack of responsibility. Chris was improving but still not very well, and needing to rest quite a lot, so I had time on my hands. Some of this time I used for going on walks. It helped me to get rid of spare energy, both physical and emotional. I have always loved walking. I think I also felt I must get myself fit in order to cope with problems later, when Chris's symptom began to return, although I hoped this might be a long time off. There were little pamphlets to be had about walks in the area, and so I put on my warm clothes, and a pair of boots, and went off. I don't know whether Chris worried about me, but she never said so. I took reasonable precautions and fortunately there were no sprained ankles. It was fun finding the way, through brambles and mud, over doubtful looking stiles, through cows and sheep, dogs barking at me, sometimes getting quite lost for a while. One path leads across an airstrip, with the directions - 'bridle path, beware low flying aircraft' and I walked across only seconds before an aircraft landed! Country living is just so different from cities. Often I would walk 6 miles across country and never see a soul. One path leads right through a deer farm, in amongst the deer and another through someone's front garden. Once I was followed by a tractor towing a spraying machine - I just hoped it wasn't toxic or blowing my way. Another time I was caught in the middle of a field in a violent thunderstorm, holding up an umbrella in torrential rain and hoping I wouldn't get struck by lightning. But I was pilgrimaging, and all sorts of things happen on a pilgrimage - part of it is reacting to the unknown. If Chris had been better I might have walked some of the Canterbury pilgrim way, but I didn't want to be far away from her or too long away. Anyway, these walks were just as good.

All the time I was also looking for the way of our pilgrimage. Soon some plans would have to be made, some decisions taken. We were using our time well; Chris was resting, writing and reading and I was walking and reading. I read Daphne du Maurier's *'Rebecca'*, and William Horwood's *'Duncton Quest'* (about handicapped moles - and by inference, people). The latter was fascinating, a fantasy about the special role of the handicapped in society, because of their different, more perceptive, way of looking at reality. I thought of stroke victims, slow learners, deaf and blind, AIDS victims, and how much we can learn from them if we only take trouble to try and communicate. A quite remarkable thing happened on March 9th. I woke having had a dream of the postman trying to squeeze a C S Lewis book through the door at Dulwich, and breaking the whole spine of the book in the process. When I got up there was a book through the door - posted to me by Valerie Rivers (who is typing this for me), by Gerard Hughes, of all people - his Lent book for last year *'Oh God, Why'* - found in a second hand shop! I was thrilled to have it, having just finished William Horwood's book the previous day. God was planning things for us again. Now I had my spiritual guidance for Lent up to Easter. I was pleased that without my planning, things were being put in place. Gerard Hughes of course, was the right author to read at this time and I kept reading bits out to Chris.

I was conscious of the fact that we were now through the time we should have been in Italy, and coming up to the Ministers conference in Eastbourne, which Chris looked as if she would be able to manage. Then there would be only a fortnight to Easter, then hopefully, it was off to Iona, and then we'd only be 10 days off the end of the Sabbatical. Should we be doing some other travelling? I asked Chris about it, she always had ideas. After all, I hoped I had plenty of life left - her life was limited, she should choose where she wanted to go.

She had lots of ideas - go and see Tim in Grimsby, see her cousin in Market Rasen - go to Bedford where Terry Waite's postcard came from - go to Turvey Abbey - to see Jan, Nigel and the new(ish) baby Jonathan (Jan is my niece) - perhaps we ought to see my Dad again. I got the map out. "Where on earth is Turvey Abbey and why do you want to go?" I said. "I've got a poster of the Black Christ in my study, from CEM days, and it's a photo of the wall-hanging in Turvey Abbey. It's near Northampton, I think. I'm sure people used to talk about it when I grew up there".

"And where are Jan and Nigel?" "In Leighton Buzzard, I think - and I say, I remember now, we had a Christmas card from Jean and Ken this year - first time for a while - and I remember their postcode is nearly the same as Jan's". Trust her to notice that and remember it.

I found Turvey Abbey on the map, near Jan's, near Jean and Ken, and near Bedford. We got in touch with Tim, but left the rest until after the ministers conference. We had to wait and see how Chris was away from the cottage, and how we coped with packing and going on a journey. Already we had been back to King's, and they had told us to pay the balance of money for Iona that was due. They must have thought that long journey was possible, so Grimsby looked as if it was on the cards. Things were working out.

That trip to King's was hectic for we just went for the day. We called in at Underhill Road to pick up the post and put the first load of washing in, then I dropped Chris and parked at Angela's. We noticed the rush and hassle. We looked at the post while we waited for the appointment, throwing the envelopes and junk mail in the bin. I'm sure we amused a lot of folk with our comments and tearing up. After seeing the registrar, who was very encouraging, and after a hospital staff lunch we went back to our Dulwich house, only to see the washing machine hadn't worked. It had to be started again. I cut the lawns, dug up plants to put in the cottage garden, and cut some more daffodil buds to take back. Chris hung out one lot of washing, put another lot in; we bagged the wet and dry stuff, and a whole lot more, and put the lawnmower in for the cottage too. We just beat the rushhour back, eating sandwiches on the way and we saw a lovely sunset. Chris was tired, but we'd done it.

During this period we managed a trip that helped to make up for not going to Italy. Before coming away, we had seen a programme on the television about the copy of the Sistine Chapel ceiling paintings, done by someone in a Roman Catholic church in a town on the South coast, which we thought was Goring. Chris's friend, who visited us from Worthing, was able to give us details, so on the actual day we should have been flying home from Italy, we set off. It was a long drive, and Chris found it hard to cope with, but she was determined to go. She had missed going to Italy more than she was prepared to admit. Her diary has lots of references to it: the day of the audience with the Pope that had been arranged for us by a local RC priest, various radio programmes she listened to that were from Italy or about it. We bought Ciabatta (Italian bread) and had minestrone soup and pasta. She was thrilled to go to a presentation of the play, Bonaventure, not just because it had been put on at Broadway Church, Walsall, by the drama group, but also because it was set in an Italian convent. She also read her diary of her visit to Italy with Helen, to visit our friends, Anna Maria and her family. She set up a photo which is one of the pilgrimage photos of the bowls of soup, the Italian diary, Anna Maria's Italian Christmas card and the programme of Bonaventure. In her diary for that day she put: "Am I getting Italy out of my system? - Yes!".

She also wrote on that date: "Read Christian's Guide to Rome - author did not like our end of the city where Hotel 'Villa Glori' was! also was quite sure we didn't need to go to Assisi to get the feel of St Francis". It was, however, very much in her mind during this period, with her vivid imagination conjuring up frescos and mosaics and set up photos.

The Church of the English Martyrs at Goring by Sea was a great treat. We sat and looked and felt ourselves in Rome, without its crowds and tourists. It was so quiet, most of the time, and we got cricks in our necks looking and marvelling. It is a superb reproduction, and just right for us as pilgrims who were denied the real thing. Chris was so excited buying lots and lots of postcards, most of which she posted off to friends just as she had posted off other Italian postcards given to us by a friend. It satisfied her to some extent. The mental imaging that was saying to her - "The cancer has not stopped me, and will not stop me. If I can't go one way I will go another. My imagination destroys the power of the cancer to deny me what I aim to do". As she would have sent postcards from Rome, so she sent them off from Goring instead.

Looking at the postcards she bought and didn't send, there is the famous picture of the creation of Adam, with the hand of God touching the hand of the newly created Adam (she kept it for her prayer corner) and I remember it had been referred to at that quiet day on November 3rd at Sayers Common. We felt the hand of God upon us as we sat in that church, glorying in the beauty of Michaelangelo's wonderful paintings (admittedly a reproduction). We were transported from the retirement town on the South coast, not only to Rome, but also to the biblical and classical conceptions of the world. What was just fantasy and unreality to some, was to us fantasy reflecting a reality far more real than the boring streets and houses outside. To pilgrims there is given a greater vision. We saw through that ceiling to God, who inspired Michaelangelo, and Gary Bevans, the signwriter who made the copy, and who was inspiring us on our pilgrimage to Rome that day.

On our journey there and back we were fortified with coffee and a piece of gateau at Sainsbury's! We ate our sandwiches outside the church in our car - not very romantic or Italian, but we made up for it one day in Hastings, being served a lovely meal Italian style. Again we could dream: you need imagination to be a pilgrim!

51

Special Times and Special Days and Special Wishes

All through our pilgrimage, and even before it began, we had lots and lots of cards and letters that helped us on our way. Several were about prayer groups that were thinking about us. One card to Chris said, "I thought I would like to write and tell you we are thinking of you. Your name is entered on our prayer list, and on Sunday evening we are having a service of healing with our Communion Service and we shall remember you in our prayers". One that Chris loved just said, "This is not a Greeting card, it's a Hug in an Envelope", and another, "We prayed for you at Thursday morning prayer today". Yet another, "We continue to pray for you at the SPCK service". One friend wrote that at her church they were remembering us both: "Our prayers are surrounding you and John at this painful time". From King's College Hospital the messages came: "We had a Ward Visitors meeting at King's today, and you were both very much in our thoughts and prayers". A surprise card came from the church where Chris was brought up, in Northampton, with a whole list of signatures, and a similar one came from the District Day at Eltham college. There were several cards recalling past events, such as "Sorry to hear of your illness. I would like to take this opportunity to thank you for your kindness in choosing my son to be the first child you christened. You made the day feel extra special and my son and I very important. May the Lord be with you". Another said, "We are all praying for you Chris, so keep that chin up, my dear". One who was going through a similar illness wrote: "Aren't our Christian friends wonderful! I really felt peace and courage and all the grace of God flowing because of the prayers and concern of other people. And God's 'own secret stair', of course - mysterious and well trodden in time of trouble". One of her church members wrote: "May the Lord God take care of you, give you a healing thought, walk with you and keep you safe. Be strong my Revd friend". A lifelong friend wrote: "I am sorry to hear of your trouble, Christine. God bless you dear and give you strength to cope". A whole church wrote a card: "We shall be thinking of you in our members meeting tonight"

Some letters and cards were very expressive of their feeling. One person, who had had cancer a few years ago wrote: "I'm so sorry. I think cancer is such a sneaky disease and have to say that my prayers at present are mixed with many angry tears. Why does it always hit the nicest people, like you? If this is not helpful to read, I apologise, but it is where I find myself, very baffled by God's ways, and I cannot manage bright platitudes. It would be good to see or speak with you sometime if you would like that, and I am still praying". One was in the form of a prayer: 'O Lord God our Heavenly Father, today I ask that you shower thy healing grace on Revd Christine, your light of thy Holy Spirit within her to renew and rebuild every cell and tissue'.

One came from America: "Received your letter and when I lit my prayer candle the next morning you both were lifted 'high to the throne of grace' - as the old hymn said. With your faith and remembering what you have told others through the years you will have the courage and hope to endure. Besides, we are people who believe in miracles. Our loving God has made promises we need to hear. We remember you well and send our love and the candle time each morning".

We both had our prayer times each day. We observed and honoured each other's privacy, so the way Chris prayed is her secret, but on previous Sundays, when we weren't both preaching, we would go together to the service, though rarely sit together as one or other of us would be taking the service. Now, at the cottage, Chris was not well enough to go, so listened to a piece on the radio while I was out at a service - usually the local CofE up on the hill.

She wrote in her diary for March 6th - "John went to church to Sedlescombe CofE. He felt very much at home - 2 Zambians there (from Pestalozzi) - a lot of women - spoke to the Rector (he liked him). People only nodded - forgot to bring me the order of service! Not as high as St John's, East Dulwich.

"I listened to Rosemary Hartill's programme for Lent, with Rabbi Lionel Blue, and Revd John Sentamu from Africa. He spoke of racial attacks he had suffered, Rabbi Blue of so much - concentration camps, Easter, he couldn't cope with - and a 20 year relationship shared, and the difficulties of the breaking up of the shared things at the end - and they tossed a coin for everything and are still friends. (He smashes plates to let it all out!). Lovely music interspersed, finishing up with Rutter's *Deep Peace of the Running Wave to You* - a lovely time of prayer and reading between them all at the end - very moving. The theme was 'Anger' and getting it out. Rabbi Blue prayed for those on AIDS wards. J is now into his old stuff again - and mowing the lawns!"

Sundays were special days and we kept them that way, but it was lovely not to have the responsibility for services. For Chris, with her time running out, and for both of us with the Sabbatical of limited length, every day was special. But some more so than others. Chris kept St David's Day with a photo of leeks and daffodils, and a comb in the shape of a Welsh lady - and Neil Kinnock with a special programme on the Radio.

Then, of course, there was Mother's Day. We celebrated twice; neither time on the correct day! The Thursday before, Sue, Simon and Matthew came. It was hot, an incredible day for early March, and we had fish and chips outside. Chris made the most of her time with her grandson again, right to the very last minute when they had to go, doing painting with him. There is a lovely photo of them both showing Matthew red-cheeked after all the fresh air running round the garden and going for a walk to see the lambs, and Chris's eyes sparkling with delight. On the Saturday Dave and Ruth came, another lovely day, but not quite so warm, and there are photos of us in the garden among the primroses, this time on our way to Bodiam Castle and a pub meal. Helen sent tome lovely flowers and, of course, there is a set up photo Chris took of her flowers and cards.

On Mothering Sunday itself both of us went to church together for the first time since our send off - to Robertsbridge URC, where there was a special preacher, the Revd Jack McKelvey, the Moderator elect of the URC. Chris knew him from student days in Nottingham and, of course, he had been Tim's principal at Northern College, so we had met at Tim's wedding. It was such a surprise to both Jack and Myrtle to see us at this little village church, they had no idea we would be there! He talked of his work in East Manchester now he was 'retired', and of suffering and obedience. Afterwards we went off with them to coffee at the manse at Sedlescombe. It was the beginning of Chris going out and meeting people again after her recuperation at the cottage. She was certainly much better and her steroids dose was now much lower, and scheduled to go right down to nothing in a fortnight's time.

We were now ready to go on our first scheduled journey, both the Fairmile Retreat and Italy having been cancelled. We were off to the Southern Province Ministers and Spouses conference at Eastbourne booked long before as part of our Pilgrimage. At last something was happening to schedule! The journeying was beginning, even though it was only a few miles away. Jack McKelvey was to be a guest speaker, which was why he was available to preach at Robertsbridge the day before.

The Conference and a Meeting

Mother's Day evening was full of packing and phone calls. All the family rang, and some friends too. Besides flowers from Helen there were some from our neighbour in memory of his wife who had died the previous year, lovely carnations from Jersey, so they had to go to Eastbourne too! We didn't have to go until the afternoon, so I had a long walk in the morning while Chris rested and got things together to go in the car. The journey was very simple, less than an hour, and Chris slept the whole way, so was refreshed and ready to meet people. It was obvious everyone was surprised at how well she was. Many people had thought we wouldn't be there. This is her diary account: "We left at 2.30 and I'm afraid I didn't see much of the journey. By 3.30 we were there, had parked and unloaded! Roy welcomed us in, amazed that we should even go!! He doesn't know me very well! Up to room - tea and lemon tea and I made it all homely and unpacked. I'm so relieved with the arrangements and no distance at all to Conference room and dining room. At 4.40 we went down for 4.45 - not overwhelming but a lot came to kiss me (hug now and then) and chat! Marion Johanson looks very poorly and frail since last time we saw her - but she isn't wearing either a wig or a scarf - I wonder why not? She and I have been naturally thrown together she is a bit confused, having convulsions and dreading chemo next. No-one seems to have explained how it is done! Jack McKelvey and Myrtle came across to talk. I shall have to learn to listen and then escape!"

I was a little apprehensive about that day, because I had been asked to lead the evening prayers. It bothered me because I'd done no leading of worship for a month, and there was a congregation entirely made up of ministers and spouses, with a moderator and URC moderator-elect thrown in! As usual, I used notes, and Chris had suggested things on the theme of 'rest' - very appropriate for being on a sabbatical. I needn't have been worried for it went well and one or two asked me where I'd got the material from.

It was Chris who was faced with the problems. The meeting of Chris and Marion was a challenge to both of them and was something God used, even if he didn't plan it. Was it coincidence that for five days two women of similar age both suffering from a brain tumour should be 'thrown together' as Chris put it? Brian, Marion's husband, had thought she might not stay at the conference at all as she was very worked up and worried about seeing people. Chris was very concerned that she didn't cover up her bald patch. Without her wig Chris looked much worse than Marion; this time her hair had gone totally, not even a wisp left. The wig was an act, but a convincing one. The two of them got on very well, and found support in each other, and Marion stayed the whole time and improved noticeably over the five days. Chris gave her a card and a scarf at the end of it. The scarf was to cover her head, but Marion put it round her neck! She wrote to Chris: "Thank you so much for your beautiful card and pretty scarf. We agree it was a wonderful week and we were so glad to get to know you a little better. We have a lot in common and I thank God for you and our mutual support. We will pray for you daily. Have a good time at Iona."

That first evening just happened to be about Christian healing, and Chris had problems with it. Brian Coward from Crowhurst spoke. Chris wrote: "He had started off gentle, but finished with scary, extreme stuff (I didn't like it)". I was doing the closing prayers but was asked if I minded if it was followed by a healing service conducted by Brian. Of course I didn't mind. Marion and Chris both agreed together to go forward for laying on of hands. Marion went first and it took a long time. Chris was agitated and whispered to me, "I don't want him to do that to me!". "You don't need to go forward", I said not knowing she'd told Marion she would. Then she saw Peter McIntosh, who was also laying on hands, and off she went to him and her diary said, "Marion was forced into a special up-front chair and they took ages - so I went to dear old Peter Mac., and a lovely quiet Scottish lady - who allowed me to say I wasn't asking for a cure -

just the strength for both of us to cope - and live full lives! Peter said there would be angels and light all along the way - she softly said all was OK! I felt healing and shalom with them." So Marion and Chris both had their own types of healing experience and all was well.

But Chris's attitude to Christian healing was a difficulty for some, and their attitude a difficulty for her, though mostly people talked to me about it rather than upsetting her. "But don't you believe in miracles, John?" some would say, when I told them she was going to die. Dulwich Grove's church magazin, *Church Echoes* was delivered to us. There was a report from the church meeting: 'There was a request from the Elders that, at 12 noon each day, we should pray that Christine should be restored to full health. The morning congregation, and indeed other groups, are being invited to join in this solidarity of prayer'. Chris read it - it was the first we knew of it - and said, "I wish they hadn't done that". I said, "At least they are all praying for you". "Yes", she said, "I'm glad about that". The problem was that she knew she would die and she was happy about it. She said so to several people and she felt people who were praying for a miracle for her were not facing her death as she was, they couldn't accept it. They were trying to force God to their way of thinking, to manipulate God to give an answer to prayer that they wanted. It was a running away from reality, living with a false hope. She wrote in her private diary that I only found after her death: "If there is suffering lying ahead be near to us all, and support John and the rest of the family! Please also support Dulwich Grove and the Elders - let them not feel let down because of their daily prayers at noon!"

That was what she was bothered about. We had heard what the doctor and the consultant had said, and we had accepted it and wanted to live the last few months. Chris didn't want to encourage in any way people thinking it might all go away with prayer, because of the effect it would have on people's faith when she died in spite of their prayer. Also, she didn't want to be distracted from facing her death by any suggestion that it might not happen if God intervened. She knew He would not intervene in this way. She was close enough to God to know that. It wasn't that she didn't believe in miracles but that the whole pilgrimage was a miracle in itself. Her whole mental imaging of her death, and the writing of her funeral, were a basis for her living and thinking herself beyond it to resurrection. The smile and the radiance came from her belief in the greatest miracle of all. From her heart there flowed this belief in the ultimate miracle. Her whole life was saying: "Death is unimportant. I have won the battle against the cancer. I will live for ever and ever." She had accepted that in her heart. Maybe intellectually I had accepted it too - but in my heart the fear of her death was very much there, and remained until the end of the pilgrimage. How could I cope without her?

For Marion it was not the same. Her cancer was different, and there was a good chance the treatment would get rid of it, at least for a while. So she was concentrating on that, and needed to ask God's help in that way. In fact, God's answer to her prayer, and the prayers of all those who asked for her physical healing, was a firm "No". Our prayers are not always answered as we want. But I am sure God brought Chris and Marion together that they might support each other at this time.

The rest of the conference was inspiring and encouraging. Each day I went off in the afternoon to walk the cliffs west of Eastbourne - Beachy Head, Birling Gap, Seven Sisters. The wind was strong, but the sun shone, and it was exhilarating. Chris would have a sleep or a quiet time then, but on one occasion in the morning took herself off on a walk to the little shops nearby. It was the first time she'd been out on her own for a long time she was thrilled, but she still felt wobbly at times. She wasn't keen on going to the talk that morning nor did she miss much! However, Jack McKelvey was brilliant, and Carmel Heaney from Belfast was good too. While we were at the conference it was St Patrick's Day. Chris took a photo of the McKelveys and Carmel to celebrate, and the prayers that evening were specially for the day. We had a really lovely time, and Chris was thrilled that her steroid dose was now very low, and she was fine -

mostly. We'd had a lot of fun and laughter, plenty of good fellowship, and some stimulating talks and services. It was tempting to think we were getting back to normality, and certainly the next stage of our pilgrimage seemed to be on. We had a lovely weekend at the cottage, doing just what we fancied. Chris was sleeping much better and nodding off in the day as well. I 'phoned Jean and Ken and they offered to put us up for a night.

I was also pleased to be able to arrange for some repairs to the cottage to be done: the rotten bits by the kitchen door and the removal of the old outside loo, to be done in Holy Week. It would just fit into our timetable nicely - everything was working out - I hoped the weather would be dry enough for the workmen and me to do some much needed outside painting too.

The Secret Garden

When we left for the cottage, Judith had provided Chris with some light reading. However, she wrote of one of them: "I finished *'Pale Battalions'* at 7.00 (am). I'm so glad I have - it was a lot to take in! a lot of characters and depravity and debauchery amongst the aristocracy, which got to me! I could only read it in the mornings, and SG as a wind-down!"

SG was her abbreviation for *'The Secret Garden'*, the children's book by Frances Hodgson Burnett. We got our copy from a second hand bookshop in Rye and we both loved reading it. It is a lovely story about the overcoming of the power of death and bereavement through the effect of resurrecting a secret garden, left locked away and forgotten; resurrected by the 'Magic' of nature. The characters, Mary the orphan girl from India, Colin the boy who was thought to be destined to be a cripple and die before he grew up, Colin's father who had locked up the garden because that's where his beautiful wife had died, and Dickon, the country boy, who loved natural things, and who was loved by birds and animals alike, were all healed in some way by the magic of the garden. In the garden Colin shouted out from his wheelchair, "I shall get well! I shall get well! Mary, Dickon, I shall get well! And I shall live for ever and ever!"

As she read that book in a morning, Chris saw the dawn coming up. She drew back the curtain at her window very early, because she found it difficult to sleep, and saw the garden - the cedar tree, the holly with its berries, the hazel catkins, and the snowdrops and primroses. She loved that garden and as long as our neighbours can remember it has always been called the 'Secret Garden'. So many people have come and commented on the feeling one gets in the garden and the cottage. One person said to me that as soon as they came in the gate, it was as if a great weight was lifted away and they could relax, and feel better. When Chris first sat in the garden she too said, "I shall get well here".

There are many connections between the book and the cottage garden: the death of Vera - just as she was about to go to the cottage; Chris being ill, and seeking to be well; the garden being overgrown, neglected, locked up and forgotten - yet full of life, just ready to come out in the Springtime and one of Chris's goals was to come to the cottage and see the primroses again. It is full of primroses everywhere, having seeded themselves, over the years. I took her photo, standing amongst them - she looks radiant.

The whole of our pilgrimage is full of springtime. Coming out of winter, life out of death, and we saw primroses everywhere we went, even on the Isle of Lewis. The *'The Secret Garden'* is about life coming out of death, and Chris and I were both facing death while looking for life and finding it, and the life overcomes the death. We did not call it the power of Magic, but the power of God. Almost every day, when Chris was resting and I had not gone for a walk, I worked in the garden, as Mary had done in the story, with Dickon helping her. I was in the business of resurrection, for years ago it had been planted with very beautiful things, and it was a question of finding them, cutting back and weeding out without destroying everything.

The hedges are such a mixture of hawthorn, beech, ivy, blackberry, ash, privet, dog-rose and more; they are a vital part of the secrecy of the garden, but cannot be allowed to grow too tall and the blackberries and ash must be got out before they take over. When I first had the cottage there was a great pile of garden rubbish right in the middle of the garden, but after removing it, the place where it was proved to be a very fertile flower bed, with delphinium 10 feet high. At the bottom of the garden are overgrown paths, overgrown with snowberry, rhododendron, japonica, mahonia, lilac and hydrangea. I didn't know where to start - it would be so easy to ruin it all by overdoing the clearing away. Then I had to be careful where I stood for there were little snowdrops as well as large ones, wood anemones and primroses everywhere. In the spring there was a succession of blossom, three apple trees in amongst the azaleas - a beautiful may tree, a lovely cherry tree, and a snowball tree so hidden you could only see it if you looked high up amongst the rest. There was so much, and much of it intertwined, asking to be given space to show itself and find the sunlight and yet if I cut too much it would spoil the whole effect. There were little flower beds to be weeded, yet even here there were bulbs to be avoided with the trowel, and deep rooted paeonies to be careful with. I found paths I didn't know existed. The water-butt was set back on its stand from where it had been thrown, and containers full of bulbs and flowers were brought from the Dulwich garden. One of the bulb containers was a 'Quality Street' tin and Chris said it pointed out our 'Quality Time' on our pilgrimage. I had inherited from the previous owner a set of slides taken at the cottage in the late sixties, to give me ideas about resurrecting it to its former glory. As the daffodils, tulips and blossom came out, so Chris and I both got stronger, and the cottage became more idyllic. Its secrecy remained - the little gate is the only way in, almost like the secret door in the book. As the Spring came, so the intensity of our living became greater. We knew this was our last Spring together - it was also my last Sabbatical. This time would never come again. It must be lived to the full - appreciated fully for what it was. We thanked God for each precious day together in such a beautiful place. That garden gate was a way into a higher plane of living or certainly symbolic of it.

The door into the secret garden in the book, and the gate off the busy road to our garden and cottage, were symbols for a way into a special spirituality where God seems very close and where events have special meanings. It is a more intense reality. C S Lewis described it in his Narnia books. There the entry was through the wardrobe, and the events that occurred were a fantasy with religious and spiritual overtones. For us, entering the pilgrimage was a kind of door, when we received our shells, but the cottage and its secret garden were allegories, or symbols, of what pilgrimage living is, and yet real too, not fantasy. But it needed the book *'The Secret Garden'* to understand the real life allegory we were living. We were really getting better, but Chris was really going to die. We needed the message of resurrection: "I shall get well. And I shall live for ever and ever". As I resurrected that garden from its neglect, and as God resurrected it with the Spring, so Chris was looking beyond death to resurrection. She said to people - "I know where I am going, and I'm happy about it but I worry about John and the family". I was doing the resurrection in the garden - I was seeing it happen. but I had not got to where Chris had. I was still deeply afraid of her death. I had a long way to go in the pilgrimage before I got rid of that fear, or could see the message portrayed by the garden. I could help God in the miracle of her resurrection, by caring for her and protecting her as she approached her death.

What we <u>do</u> in a pilgrimage is important for what it means in a spiritual sense. The meaning may not be fully apparent at the time - or even apparent at all.

We were going through the season of Lent. Lent stands on its own, yet can also be thought of as a preparation for Easter. So my labour in the garden stood on its own - it was something that needed doing to bring out the full wonder of the Spring garden, but it was also my preparation for my own Easter, when Good Friday would be Chris's death, and Easter Sunday my realisation of her resurrection. My seeing the daffodils, primroses and blossom was a preparation for my really seeing her resurrection, and the book *'The Secret Garden'* helped both of us to see that death can be overcome. Our other secret garden helped us to see <u>how</u>, as the book's 'secret garden' had helped the children to see <u>how</u>.

God was leading us through our pilgrimage - of that we were in no doubt - and we had plans and He had plans. He helped us achieve something of our Italian plans, through Chris's determination not to be totally cheated. He added the secret garden to our plans, and in many ways *made* it the heart of our pilgrimage, though we were not aware of it at the time. But in that little children's, book death and resurrection are the theme of a simple story, and as we read it and became like children, the garden shone with God's glory, and the weight on us - me especially - of Chris's terminal cancer and its consequences, was lifted, and our eyes could sparkle with resurrection hope.

Little things in the garden became important because they were also in the book: the trailing ivy, the festoons of roses over the archway, the badger digging up the lawn, the squirrel playing in the trees and most of all, the robin. It came close to me when I was digging or weeding and it came up to the cottage window where Chris was sitting. It was as if it was the same one who in the book showed Mary the door and the key. It was as if we were living in a fantasy world - but then, why not? Little children do and who is to say that their view of the world is less valid than ours.

The Little Journey

The Sunday was a lovely spring day after a bit of frost. We'd both slept well, and the sun shone strongly on to us as we ate our breakfast. I went off to the Parish church, walking up the hill past gardens full of spring flowers, the blackthorn out in the hedgerows, and the birds in full song. People at the church were friendly, the vicar asking me if I'd be at the church the next Sunday, but we had other plans. I think he wanted me to do a reading and it felt good to feel wanted and noticed. As I walked back I felt Spring had really come - the first day of Spring was actually the next day. The garden was growing apace and I did quite a lot of hedge-trimming discovering more types of plants in it - more japonica, kerria, rhododendron and trailing roses. What a beautiful place. I took Chris's photo standing amongst the primroses in the sunshine. She was well enough to cook the midday meal and in the afternoon we went to the beach - there was a cool wind, not sitting out weather, but still very beautiful. We came back past fields of spring lambs, and took their photographs. It was a special day. Chris had listened to Rosemary Hartill on the radio talking about stress and we felt very wound down. Chris was only a week away from finishing with the steroids altogether, and she was sleeping well, relaxing, no longer 'hyper'. In the evening we confirmed arrangements for going to Grimsby and coming back via Leighton Buzzard.

We got up early the next day for our little pilgrimage. Going to see Tim was very important. Whenever Chris talked about her 'goals' his ordination seemed always to be the last one. She had said, "I can see myself into June - it is more difficult to think myself into July", but recently she was saying she could get herself to Tim's ordination on July 30th, but it was difficult. She had been very excited about the news of the first CofE women's ordinations at Bristol just 9 days before and there is a special entry in her diary. I'm sure in her mind Tim being ordained somehow compensated for her having to give up. It was a long journey but we had no problems. We had a coffee stop at Thurrock. Chris said, "Is that peacock stuffed?" It was a picture painted on the wall but she was convinced it was a stuffed bird - she had a sensation of 3D about it and had to go up to it to realise she was wrong; just a little reminder that all was not as it should be with her. It was sunshine all the way, and Chris cat-napped, but was excited at seeing Lincoln cathedral. She had taught in the girls' school close to the cathedral for two years - one of the themes of the pilgrimage - a going back in time in her life. Eventually we found Tim's flat. He hadn't warned us of very awkwardly placed roadworks. He got a shock at how slow Chris was getting up the stairs which we found out later is a side effect of steroid treatment. In the evening we had a long chat about the four churches in Huddersfield which Tim would take over, together with his colleague already there. We were all very excited about it. Tim and Rebekah tried to describe what the Manse was like, and the alterations they were doing for them, especially in the kitchen which was small. Both of them had their courses to finish, Tim doing his dissertation and Rebekah with just over a term to do with teaching practice, so they were both very busy.

It so happened that Rebekah's father, Rodney Ward, had taken over part of an ecumenical officer's job when he took on as minister at Gainsborough and the person from whom he took over, Revd Geoff Towell, was a long lost cousin of Chris's! So the next day we went to see him at Market Rasen, just a few miles away. He has MS and is in a wheelchair, but is very active and on various committees. His wife was out, but we found she had left everything ready for coffee, and we had a very pleasant time. We had met briefly before at Rodney's induction. I listened as they talked of times way back, and Chris looked at paintings hanging up that she remembered seeing before. It was a delving back over forty years. They talked, too, of Geoff's sister Janet, married to a CofE priest in Manchester, whom I had met nearly 30 years earlier and with whom Chris was still in contact. We all talked about our work as ministers in city and country. As we left and goodbyes were said Geoff and Chris realised, I am sure, that they were unlikely to see each other again - but such meetings were important. Part of the pilgrimage was making or renewing contact and saying goodbye. But there were never any heart-rending scenes - always Chris was cheery and positive - I never dreaded the goodbyes.

We went back through the Lincolnshire wolds with daffodils but no primroses, and thought of Simon's parents not far away. When we got to the flat Chris went to bed and slept the afternoon away while I went with Tim for a walk round the docks, bringing back memories of his work with the Seamen's Mission. Now he was to take on ordinary parish work. He'd never thought he would do it always feeling thet he would be happier in a chaplaincy. It was good to be together, both of us looking into an uncertain future, wondering whether we'd be able to cope in our different ways. We picked up some shells on the beach, which would go into my collection of souvenirs. The next day we had to leave. Rebekah left early for school and Tim had his dissertation to finish, and we wound our way through pretty countryside for a while before the busy roads took us to Bedford on our way to Turvey. Chris was excitedly showing me roads she recognised from childhood visits - she'd never been back since - going over from her home town, Northampton, to visit an uncle and aunt in Bedford. "Can we see Bunyan Meeting?" she said. "Where is it?" I asked. "Somewhere in the middle of Bedford", she said! In normal times we would not have found it. It's a big place and we'd have got lost. But this was a pilgrimage and God was leading us. "I'll try down here", I said. "There it is", said Chris - but it wasn't, it was a Roman Catholic church. "No", I said, "it's not here - I'll have to turn round and go back". I went down a side-street to turn and there it was, or rather, the back of it. I parked, tried to get in, but it was all closed. I didn't realise I was at the back. "Sorry", I said to Chris, "all shut up, I'm afraid". We drove off, got lost, and suddenly she said, "There it is - the front of it - and it's open." I parked just by at some business premises - yellow lines everywhere - just room for me 10 yards from the entrance. We were both convinced we were meant to find it: God had led us there. It was an uncanny feeling, but we often felt it on this pilgrimage, everything worked out - it wasn't possible, and then suddenly it was, all in a moment.

We went in through doors depicting the *'Pilgrim's Progress'* - we, too, were pilgrims. We looked round and gazed at the window depicted on Terry Waite's postcard. Here was a theme Chris had latched onto through reading *'Cancer Ward'*: prison - and the spirit going out from the prison, escaping into imagination: Bunyan in his cell with a pen in his hand beginning to write. The first words are written around the window: "As I walked through the wilderness of this world I lighted on a certain place where there was a den, and laid me down in that place to sleep, and as I slept I dreamed a dream". To how many people has that dream brought inspiration and spiritual understanding over the years? Yet Bunyan wrote it confined to prison, his imagination giving him freedom, maybe inspired by Paul writing his letters in prison. Terry Waite looked at the postcard and envied the pen and paper, and the view through the bars of the window, yet wrote his book in his head because there was nowhere else he could. And Solzenitzin's Oleg dreamt of an apricot tree as he was in 'prison' in hospital. Chris, too, had been set free as a pilgrim for a little while. Would she be able to fly, as the eagle from London Zoo did in William Horwood's book, to the stones of Callanish? Would she be strong enough to go back, as the eagle did, to the place of captivity to tell others of the way to freedom, and the power of freedom?

I'm sure we didn't think all this as we walked around the church taking photos, having a cup of tea and buying souvenirs, but the connections are all there, and part of the wonder of a pilgrimage is to see its meaning afterwards. The amazing thing is that when we set off from Grimsby we had no real idea of going to Bunyan Meeting. We knew the way to Turvey went through Bedford, but we didn't think we had time to do anything about Bunyan. God knew otherwise.

Our next step was Turvey Abbey - very much a mixture of old and new. It is a Benedictine community and is famous for its wall hangings. We hadn't told them we were coming but, of course, they were very welcoming. Two nuns looked after us and showed us round, but were puzzled by Chris asking to see the wall hanging of the black Christ.

On the wall of Chris's study in East Dulwich is a black Christ hanging on a cross, and the acknowledgement is 'Turvey Abbey'. For a long time there was a feeling of disbelief by the nuns. They showed us posters of wall hangings and then Chris said, "That's it!" "Oh, the Risen Christ, you mean", they said, "but Christ isn't black, he's brown". The poster Chris had was very dark, but their poster was full of colour, and the idea of Christ rising from the cross itself is there. "Can I see the wall hanging itself?" asked Chris. "Well, no, I'm afraid not. It is only shown from Easter Day to Pentecost. Come back then". Well, of course, she never saw it, but she bought another poster of it with 'He is Risen' written on it, and put it up at the cottage on Easter Day. The symbolism of what we thought was crucifixion turning into resurrection is very apt. I also bought a poster of a Pentecost wall hanging, the wind and the flame, to give to Dulwich Grove church on Pentecost Sunday when we got back, and which remains on the wall in the sanctuary now. The nuns showed us an enormous wall hanging on the theme of water: from the chaos of creation, through Noah, the Red Sea, Water from the Rock, to the baptism of Jesus, the water from his side at the crucifixion, and the river of the water of life from Ezekiel and Revelation. I was reminded of the mosaic in King's College Hospital chapel of the Holy City and the river flowing from it. I have looked at it so many times waiting for Chris to finish her chaplaincy work, or when I have gone in to pray while she was having treatment or tests, or more recently preparing to go on my rounds as a chaplain.

We were told that we could look round the gardens if we wished. The spring flowers were so beautiful - a real haven of peace and tranquillity - so unexpected: daffodils, polyanthus, violets, scillas and blue wood anemones, with a lovely sweet smelling shrub perfuming everywhere; and a wonderful Easter garden, there all the year round - quite large. There was a pool, and round it the stations of the cross, and at the end the three crosses and the empty tomb. I was really enthralled with it - a lovely thing to remind us that our pilgrimage through Lent would lead in 4 days' time to Palm Sunday, Good Friday and Easter Day. It also reminded us that the message of Easter is for every day, and that crucifixion and resurrection are to be celebrated always, not just at Easter.

After that Milton Keynes with its grid system and concrete cows was totally uninspiring, but we did go through Olney and thought of John Newton and William Cowper, but didn't feel like stopping. We found the lovely thatched cottage belonging to our friends, Jean and Ken at Stewkely and all of us were taken back 17 years or so since we last met. Ken was one of my elders in Broadway Church, Walsall, and helped with the young people's group on a Sunday. He has worked with the Open University for many years in metallurgy and is a wizard at making things work, from cars to plumbing, electric's to construction and carpentry. The thatched cottage had his hallmark all over it, and it was fascinating. Jean, a health visitor now retired, is so interested in people, and it was as if the years had fallen away and we'd just slipped back in time. It was a wonderful time - so short - just an evening, a night, and a morning. Such is the way of pilgrimages and we had to move on. I went off for a morning walk, and when I got back Jean and Chris were still talking away.

But this was to be a moving on kind of day, first to my niece's for lunch. Christopher, her eldest, was doubtful at first, but eventually was calling me 'Grandpa', and the baby was gorgeous (first time we'd seen him). Janice remarked that w were 'Chris and John' and her two children were Christopher and Jonathan, we'd never thought of that. Chris had a long sleep after lunch and had to be woken because we were off to Mill Hill to see my father and Mabel for tea. We didn't realise it then, but it was to be Chris's last visit, though of course we were in touch often by 'phone. Because of the pilgrimage, we would not be able to go again until after mid-May, and by then Chris was not well enough. As it was, the journey across London to East Dulwich was pretty stressful, though Chris dozed for much of the way. That evening (what was left of it - we got back at 10 pm) and the following day we were very busy trying to get everything done: seeing the neighbours, doing the washing, watering plants, sorting out the post, repacking, seeing my church secretary, shopping. Eventually, the following evening we set off for the cottage, only to go back after getting a mile up the road - we'd left some things in the fridge, but at 9 o'clock we were back and we unpacked most things. We'd managed the little journey!

Holy Week and Easter

The following day Chris woke with a bad headache, the first for a very long time. Was it reaction to the journey or something more sinister? Whatever it was, it went off gradually. Helen had sent me some cottage garden seeds, so I planted them in a space I had cleared, and some others I had too. The others were no good at all, but later Helen's came up beautifully. Spring was definitely here. I went on a walk and took photos of the wild flowers and blossom. Chris had a flower arrangement in a basket through Interflora from her old church in Northampton, Doddridge Memorial. It was a lovely thought for Easter, and Chris rang them up and had a long chat, she was very thrilled. We had a meal out and went to a concert in Bexhill. It was a lovely day after all.

Summertime clockwise started overnight so it was a bit of an effort to get off for our special Palm Sunday idea. We thought we would join (or watch) the procession advertised in Bexhill, but we never found it, just a few stalwarts holding palms, braving the cold wind at what we thought was the wrong place. We never found the church either, so eventually found ourselves at St Peter's in the Old Town. We'd been there before and Chris had noticed the St Perpetua chapel that reminded her of Perpetua Head near Florence in Oregon, so named as it was sighted by Captain Cook on St Perpetua Day. The service was half over, but at least we got there for the Palm Sunday hymns and communion. It was crowded out - we were served communion by two ladies which Chris liked especially. The choir sang 'All for Jesus' from Stainer's crucifixion which had Chris reaching for her hankie, and we were given palm crosses. It was very beautiful and full of life - obviously a very busy church. We had missed a reading of the Passion story, but it was good to be in a crowd on <u>Palm</u> Sunday, joining in and trying to find out what was going on - very suitable. In the afternoon Chris proved she could take a walk, just a short one, but she managed it with a sit down in the sun. We met lots of people who were pleased to see her managing to get about a bit on her feet. It's a lovely friendly village, and everyone was very encouraging - they all knew the situation. On Monday we prepared for Easter Day with a "trial run". I felt it was important to time our journey to Canterbury Cathedral, find out about the best car park, and make sure of the right service so as to hear the Archbishop. I didn't want a repeat performance of yesterday, which turned out well but was not what we wanted at Easter. We had a great day, starting with coffee at Tenterden, and a big meal in a Canterbury restaurant before getting to the Cathedral which was crowded with tourists. I got the information I wanted: the service with the Archbishop would be at 11 am. Chris wanted to find the Christkindl market and we found it eventually. She was hankering after a clock for her birthday, but that day we only bought some Christmas serviettes (they went down on my 'how to do Christmas' instructions!). Then Chris had a long rest in the Roman Catholic St Thomas's church, much more peaceful than the cathedral, and while she was there I bought her an Easter card and present from the Christian bookshop - *'The Curate's Awakening'* by George McDonald. I was very pleased to find it, and hoped she would like it. Then we had very expensive hot chocolate piled up with cream in a cafe called Il Vaticano: the Vatican as well as the Sistine chapel! A lovely day; and we celebrated Chris taking her last steroid tablet, according to the consultant's orders.

On Tuesday we had a restful day. Chris slept right on till nearly 9 o'clock - quite unheard of recently. We got back the photos of our 'little journey' and were very pleased with them. I was out clearing things away ready for the builders coming the next day and went off to the tip with a lot of junk. Chris admits in her diary to being very lethargic and boring to be with, but she still did a lot of ironing! I was beginning to think of the long journey to Iona and beyond, and 'phoned Ian at Callanish, Isle of Lewis. He was really excited - yes, the dates I had in mind were fine. He was obviously prepared to put himself out considerably for us, it was lovely hearing his broad Scots accent from so far away, and in the background the noise of the children larking about. I wondered whether our visit could possibly happen for Chris was a bit unsteady, sleepy, and had a cough.

On Wednesday the builders arrived very early. I wasn't up and Chris wasn't even awake. We called them the 'woodmen' because they were brothers and their name was 'Wood'! - and, of course, the cottage is wooden. They had done work at the cottage before. Much of what they did had been recommended by the person who did the survey on the cottage before we bought it, but this was the first opportunity to get it done. A lot of it was rot and cracked and flaking concrete, and the removal of the outside loo which was no longer connected to the water supply, and led into the old cess pit at the bottom of the garden. Of course it was a bigger job than they had thought (isn't it always!). I left them prising and splitting off the wood and hoping they knew what they were doing, and went inside for breakfast to find Chris in trouble. Her balance was funny and she found it difficult to get out of bed without falling back. She also had a bit of backache and was very sleepy. I went down to the surgery to seek advice from the local doctor - we had registered with them previously - and I took the letter from King's College Hospital to let them know about Chris's condition. He suggested going back on the steroids, a dose of 8 times what she had recently been having. It seemed a bit drastic so Chris decided to take just 4 times the dose and see what happened. She stayed very sleepy but wrote lots of letters. I posted 11 for her at the end of the day. In the evening we listened to the radio, and Chris loved the 'St Matthew Passion' from King's College, Cambridge. She wrote in her diary: "I love that incredibly poignant note on which the last chorale 'Tears of Grief' ends - it has promise, grief, disappointment and anger somehow all represented there!" Did that reflect her mood, I wonder? Was she thinking the cancer was going to cheat her out of Iona and Callanish after all? We didn't talk about it. The rain came down, and we said how lucky it was it had been dry all day for the woodmen, and how hard they had worked. I worked out possibilities for the Iona/Callanish trip with the aid of a ferry timetable, so that at any point we could turn back if Chris was not fit. I was aware that the distances were very large. I had an evening walk - short and brisk - making the most of the longer daylight, and trying to get rid of my anxious feelings about Chris.

So we came to Maundy Thursday, and we thought of other Maundy Thursdays over the years. I felt very strange not to be preparing a service, and remembered with pleasure the services in the upper room in Moseley - the foot washing, the Jewish passover table, the service of Tenebrae. It was a lovely room to be in at that service. Chris remembered Elsie from St John's, so proud of her Maundy money received from the Queen one year, and the joint service at Camberwell Green with Dulwich Grove, moving from one room to another. As the woodmen worked outside, so we listened to the Royal Maundy service from Truro cathedral. It was very traditional, and it was interesting to hear about some of the recipients of the money. In spite of an early shower, the weather stayed dry enough for the work outside to be finished by lunchtime. I was really pleased with what they'd done, and did an afternoon's painting, while Chris baked her Colomba for Easter (a Colomba is a cake made specially for Easter in Italy and Chris had the recipe from her visit to Anna Maria some years ago). She was obviously feeling better but with rain and strong winds coming in the evening we decided not to go to the URC at Robertsbridge for the evening service. As Chris put in her diary: "How lovely (on a sabbatical - and illness as an excuse) to be able to be like everyone else in your congregation, and decide not to go!" Ian 'phoned again with some more ideas for getting to Callanish! He was getting us excited too, and determined we would not be put off if we could help it.

Good Friday has never been Chris's favourite day. I went off to Sedlescombe URC and the service was taken by lay people, with a beautiful sung solo by Marie, their organist who has a lovely voice. She gave a little talk, too. Afterwards there were hot cross buns and coffee.

I walked back, disdaining a lift from Marie, and just avoided getting soaked by a shower by going in the Post Office. Chris listened to the radio meditation by Father Oliver McTernan and to a children's story, and then made some Easter biscuits. Strange she could face her own death, but has always found the crucifixion day very difficult. Perhaps the suffering of Christ was what she couldn't cope with. I gave her her Easter card and present and she was thrilled with both - the card had primroses and other spring flowers in the shape of a Celtic cross. I finished off my painting outside, and then the wind and rain came again, but we went to the Easter music concert at Bexhill even so, Chris hanging onto her wig! It was good, but a bit churchy, if you know what I mean! We saw several people we knew there.

Easter Saturday was a day of very heavy showers, one moment it was sunny, and the next black as ink and pouring with heavy hail, but it didn't matter. Chris was sorting out the cooking and I set off to get some shopping for her. I had just got back when friends arrived with flowers and I left them talking to Chris while I went off to met Helen at Battle station. She brought lots of flowers too - so Chris had masses all over the cottage.

Helen brought presents, and it was lovely to see her and chat about her holiday in Derbyshire. We just talked and talked, and then Chris and she were in the kitchen cooking, just like old times. After the meal, we sat by a lovely fire watching some slides on the screen during which Chris fell asleep, and we were all very happy. It was going to be a special Easter for all of us, and we just hoped arrangements would work out for Easter Day, a day we had planned for so long. I finished Gerard Hughes book for Lent, though I felt I had rather rushed through the first part.

And so the great day arrived, planned originally to be at Iona. Chris's alarm went off at 3.30 am! Fortunately only she heard it. We got up at 7.30, to sunshine at first, a perfect Easter morning. Of course we had boiled eggs for breakfast, and I drew a face on Chris's, just as I had done over the years for the children on Easter morning. The sun poured into the cottage, and the garden we looked out on was full of beautiful spring flowers. Easter is about early morning, and gardens and gardeners. Off we went, three pilgrims, to Canterbury, as so many have over the years. It was a good quick journey and Chris made up for her very early start! We parked where we had planned, and walked through the beautiful gardens to the cathedral enjoying magnolia, spring bulbs, primulas and blossom. The sun shone and everything seemed to sparkle with delight on this special day. We were really excited, and joined the other pilgrims making their way to the cathedral door. Chris was unsteady, holding on to Helen's arm as I took photos. In the sanctuary itself all was expectation and there were beautiful Easter lilies near the font. We got rather poor places at the side, but then people were moved into reserved seats that were still empty at the last minute, and we took their places, quite close to the pulpit with an excellent view. The TV cameras were there, and the choir sang, their voices floating round the nave. Then the Archbishop entered and shouted: "The Lord is Risen" and there was a great roar: "He is risen indeed". It was a moment when my blood tingled with excitement. What a privilege to be there. The reading from *Colossians 3* was so apt for us: "You have been raised to life with Christ so set your hearts on the things that are in heaven. Keep your minds fixed there, not on things here on earth. For you have died and your life is hidden with Christ in God. Your real life is Christ". Gerard Hughes wrote in *'Oh God Why'* for Easter Sunday "Belief is knowing, but a knowing which is not based solely on observation, inner reasoning, logical deduction, or the assurance of other people. Belief is an inner sensing, more like an intuition". In that cathedral that morning it seemed to me impossible not to believe in the resurrection. Christ was there with us. God had led us to this holy place.

The sermon was wonderful, full of the Easter message. We saw the Archbishop first coming down the aisle in procession, and then were able to see him quite close as he prepared himself and ascended the pulpit steps. Chris was worried that she was too unsteady to go forward to receive communion, but she managed it. We shared the peace after the words "The risen Christ came among his disciples and said 'Peace be with you'. Then they were glad when they saw the Lord". It was a great climax in our pilgrimage.

We stayed for a while afterwards. Helen walked round the cathedral and I took photos - Chris just took in the scene. Then we walked away looking for a place for a meal. Chris couldn't walk far, but Helen's sharp eyes saw the Queen Elizabeth's Guest Chamber. We found a table and looked at the ancient decorated ceiling and read the history. It was a lovely Easter meal, a turkey special, in a place frequented by pilgrims down the ages (part of the old Crown Inn). We talked about the service, and I said, "I suppose the sermon could have been construed to be partly political". Later when we heard the radio and read the papers, we were amazed. "Carey's message is one salvo in the 15 year war between church and Tory state" - nothing about the Easter message. Had we attended the same service as the reporters? They did not sense the wonder of Easter. It is not 'news'! Going out into the sunshine again to make our way back, we took a different route, being rewarded by a fabulous view across Romney Marsh. Coming past Sedlescome Parish church I took a photo of its lovely Easter garden with primroses and other spring flowers. As we got back to the cottage it began to rain, but it didn't matter. We had trifle as a dessert and lit the Norwegian candles we had, ate some Colomba and some Easter eggs and Chris took a photo of our Easter table. In the evening we went to a little Easter hymn-sing over the road at the village hall, and met up with a number of friends. We got soaked going and coming back but it didn't matter, people were so helpful, bringing us cups of tea and cakes - profiteroles and buns. In bed that night Chris read from *'The Cross of Life'* picked up at Oberammergau. The author, Theodor Glaser, writes: "I want nothing to do with this crazy world of ours, with its strategies of death: I want to get out in search of God's crazy world with its strategies of life. But we needn't wait for our death before we can enjoy the true life. That is God's affair, anyway, in the world beyond. Our business is to live in this world before we die, to be viable and strong and courageous and worthy of life. Easter is God's way of saying "Yes" to life".

As I wrote in my diary, "A truly memorable Easter -
a goal of our pilgrimage well and truly achieved".
And Chris put up her poster from Turvey Abbey - 'He is Risen'.

PART III
THE LONG JOURNEY AND ON TO PENTECOST

Preparations

There were just 9 days to go before we planned to start up North. The main concern was Chris's health. We had had to put up her steroid dose again to the level originally suggested by the local doctor. I was pretty worried what the consultant at King's would say. It was on the Wednesday after Easter that we had the journey back to London for the appointment. We had a long wait, and were able to open our post collected from the Dulwich house. There were lots of Easter cards, many from Chris's church at Camberwell Green. Eventually we had the interview, and I was relieved. We had got the all-clear for Iona and Callanish! I was given charge of the steroid dose, but was told it was unlikely I need alter it much. Basically, the hospital were pleased at how things were going. While we were in London I had a frantic time putting the garden to rights, and Chris was helped by Tim and Rebekah (who were there for a holiday) doing loads and loads of washing. I brought yet more plants back for the cottage garden.

Then there was the car to sort out. It needed two new front tyres, and I asked the garage to look and see if they could find the source of a strange knocking sound, a bit like a brake catching. They did a good check up, and decided everything was fine after a few adjustments.

I rang Iona to confirm everything was fine, and told them of Chris's state of health. They agreed to do all they could to help and advised me to book the ferry, which I did. In fact I spent a long time with maps and the diary, trying to sort out our plans. It was a question of connecting with the ferries, and not having so much driving that Chris couldn't cope. Chris sorted out the packing, as she always did. She was not at all keen on living out of suitcases and liked to get somewhere, unpack and stay there. But a pilgrimage is moving around, and she tried to pack so that essential things were easily accessible, and planned that at Iona and Callanish there would have to be a complete unpack and re-sort.

During this time we visited some neighbours for the first time - so strange that both our closest neighbours have lived in Dulwich, and we went to see a play - a Francis Durbridge thriller.

After the excitement of Easter, and all its spiritual meanings, this took on the feel of an ordinary holiday, but we were excited, and a little apprehensive about the long journey ahead. We were free to go, and that was wonderful. But would we cope with the fairly taxing schedule? We had been to Iona before - me three times, Chris twice, but this time it was a part of a larger pilgrimage. What would it mean to us?. And what would we make of the mysterious stones at Callanish?

It was as if the cloud was settled over the tent for a while, and we wanted to move, but we weren't totally sure where it would take us, and why. There was also the sense that we could begin to see the end of the sabbatical, and didn't want to. Perhaps also there was a feeling that Chris was coming to what would be her last journey. Even on her higher steroid dose she was finding it difficult to balance, and increasingly difficult to climb up steps. Easter was such a climax that there was bound to be a reaction, I suppose, but I think more than anything, for both her and for me in different ways, there was a feeling that we had a glorious freedom to come, but it would only be for so long, and then would come the hard struggle to cope, with circumstances again constraining us.

It's interesting to read our diaries side by side at this period. Chris's diary never mentions that on the Saturday and Sunday mornings there was heavy snow - perhaps she didn't want to see it for she hated snow, and by the time she got washed and dressed most of it had gone. Her diary is full of the visit to the neighbours, the meals we had, and all the packing. There's only the slightest mention of the car's tyres and servicing, added as an afterthought. It was because we were so different that we worked so well as a team. I never gave it a thought that we would forget anything in the packing. I just knew she did not forget, and trusted her entirely. Maybe this too was a worry; I was no doubt wondering how I would cope when she couldn't do it. We relied on each other a great deal. Thank goodness she wrote a diary, or much of what I am writing here could not have been written, the memories would have died with her.

I had worked out that we needed four nights in order to get to Iona. I daren't make the journeys any longer in time than the one we had made to Grimsby, because I felt Chris couldn't cope with anything lengthier. We had arranged the first night at my Aunt's in Wakefield, but nothing after that. It was early in the season and I trusted there'd be plenty of bed and breakfast places available. Before we left on the Tuesday, we spent a long time on the 'phone to family and friends. I think everyone was a bit worried about how we would manage the journey, but very glad we were able to go. We felt a lot of prayers were being said for us realising how important this journey was for us.

On the Sunday, Chris listened to her radio - from 'Spring Harvest' at Minehead - with music conducted by Graham Kendrick while I went with the people from next door to Sedlescombe Parish Church. The vicar, Colin, talked about food and manna and bread for eternal life - very suitable for someone on pilgrimage, as the Israelites were pilgrims in the desert wilderness. Chris rang our friend at Wigan and it was fine to stop there for Wednesday lunch.

So on the Monday night the cottage had been cleaned, the food eaten up, the gardens put to rights, the car sorted out, and the bags and cases were ready to load up: two cases for Iona and Callanish, an overnight bag, knitting bag, King's College Hospital bag, green bag, laundry bag, boots, coats. And Chris wrote a stinker of a letter to the catalogue place who still hadn't sent her primrose dress (her gown of glory!).

It was a great feeling of anticipation, but I think we both knew it was the last time we would be packing up like this to go on a journey together. We prayed it would work out, after so much planning.

On the Way to Iona

Chris wrote in her diary for Tuesday: "J called me at 7.30 - cold and frosty - as usual! So didn't want to get out, except that it was the start of an adventure! Listened to Thought for the Day - Omar Haggadus with two teeth extraction's! Yesterday it was Pauline Webb on crutches! What a lot!"

The morning was lovely and sunny, and the garden looked beautiful as I walked through it with cases and bags, after breakfast at our sunny window. We were both very excited. Two months' ago this would have been quite impossible, but now it was happening. We had been waiting for the cloud to move, for the Holy Spirit to empower us. This was what we had planned ages ago - in fact, well over a year ago. Why was it so important to go to Iona? The wind blows, the dove flies, the wild goose goes free, and Callanish was the place of the eagle, the symbol of strength and freedom for us. Chris's illness would not have its way - not yet. It could not stop us now, we were sure of that. We felt the power of God pushing us forward.

As the Secret Garden was about resurrection, so this journey was about the Holy Spirit's power. Columba set sail from Ireland letting the wind and waves take him to a distant place, and God sent him to Iona. We as pilgrims were going to Iona too, and to the more distant, wild and bleak Western Isles, with so many mixed thoughts. We could not have explained why we were going, but for both of us it was very important, not least as a final achievement together.

There was nothing particularly romantic about the journey up to Wakefield. There were traffic jams where I had not expected them. After the sunny beginning it began to rain. Chris slept quite a lot of the way as usual, but I was seriously worried about the car. It was fine at first, but then it seemed as if a brake was catching somewhere on the front wheel. It seemed to be at certain speeds, and at certain positions of the steering. I could feel a very slight jarring on the steering wheel, and then in the traffic jam it became worse - scrape, scrape, creak, groan. What on earth was it? The garage had looked at it and said all was well, so I tried not to bother about it. We couldn't afford the time for it to go in a garage again and in any case it only happened sometimes. But faults in cars get worse and we had a long way to go. Was this to test our faith? Doris in Wakefield was pleased to see us and loved the flowers Chris had taken her. We were a bit later than we'd said - partly the traffic - partly the restaurant's slow service for lunch near Grantham. She had hoped we'd be able to see her on the little journey but it was too far. She was so pleased to be part of this journey. We shared some of her birthday cake with her (from three weeks before) and she lit a candle for us. We showed her the photos of the Pilgrimage so far. My Dad 'phoned, and of course he would have to mention the car. "Is it up to the journey?" he asked, "have you had it serviced?" "Going beautifully", I said, "it's fine", and then I had a sleepless night worrying about it. So much for my faith! We heard the weather forecast and it seemed good for the next day or two on the Western side where we were going.

Doris lives next to the council depot, and the hooter goes at 7.30 a.m., so we didn't have to set an alarm. Chris was up quickly, and we were ready to leave by 9.00. We had worried about Doris's steep stairs, but Chris managed fine and to save another climb up for the loo, we stopped for petrol close by where there was a handy place! Stairs were getting to be quite a problem. Half-way over the Pennines I suddenly thought of my camera. I'd got it out to take a photo of the cat, and put it down on a chair. I was sure I'd left it there. But you can't do U turns on the M62 and we were well into Lancashire before I could stop and look. It was there! Thank Goodness! I was in a pretty anxious state!

Miraculously as it seemed to me, we found Sydney's house in Wigan straight away. Every other time we've spent half a hour looking and asking. He was all ready for us, and after coffee he said, "Now Chris, you're going to ring Kathleen in Newfoundland. It's all set up - have a good chat". And she did - for about half an hour. Sydney insisted the cost didn't matter at all. Of course, it would be the last time - we realised that later - as it was the last time Doris saw Chris too. Expense has no importance at these times.

We went and saw the garden - over 3,000 daffodils, and all at their best, it seemed. We had come on just the right day, with the sun shining on them all, leading down to the lake at the bottom of the garden. He plants them each year individually, and this year it seemed he had planted them all especially for that day. It was surely not a coincidence they were just perfectly out or that the sun shone. They were praising God in their beauty, and we thanked God for his kindness to us. We had lunch together at the table in the window looking out at them, and we recalled memories of years ago, including our wedding when Kathleen was one of the bridesmaids, and Sydney had given a speech. As with the little journey, so this was partly a going back in time for us, especially for Chris - the Leighs and her family had had many, many happy holidays together. But we had to get on. Off we went past Preston and Lancaster. The motorway went close to the house where we'd stayed on holiday, by Farleton Fell. I remembered climbing the fell before breakfast each morning with some of the children, and the good food we'd had there. But Chris was asleep! And then I saw them. The air was as clear as a bell, and there were the Lake District mountains, far away in snow! "Look," I said excitedly to Chris, "the Lakes - look at the snow!" She struggled to wake up. "Is that all", she said, "What did you wake me for? I was having a lovely sleep". She put in her diary: "J woke me up to see snow! It did look nice! But I could have done without it".

We stopped for the night at Pooley Bridge as I had planned, getting a bedroom with a fabulous view of the bridge and the snow-covered mountains over Ullswater. They gave us tea, and were very friendly. We had time for a drive to Martindale and went into the church there, trying to remember when it was we had visited before, on holiday with the family. Chris remembered her youth hostelling days in the lakes with her student friends from Nottingham University. She wasn't much of a walker, but they always wanted her to go, and often she would hitch-hike up from Northampton in safer days than now. She recalled the day when she got stuck on Striding Edge - she was never one for heights, and her nerve failed completely. Patient persuasion eventually got her across. Memories, memories! In her diary she said: "I listened to the silence".

That evening I left her looking at the view, while I went for a walk down to the lake, and then by the river amongst the sheep and lambs. What a lovely place to be in Springtime in such glorious weather. I felt relaxed and confident. In spite of the creaks and grinds, the car had gone up and down hairpin bends to Martindale with no trouble at all, so surely there could be nothing seriously wrong. I would not spoil this wonderful time by worrying. I breathed in the fresh clean air and felt totally exhilarated. As we made our evening drinks in the bedroom it reminded us of other holidays, and we laughed and joked together, and our troubles were completely forgotten. "But all shall be well, and all shall be well, and all manner of things shall be well" as Mother Julian said. And Chris's comment in her diary was, "Nice little friendly B&B. Knitted and did 4 p/c's. Cocoa and choc break mixed. Bed - lovely double!"

The next morning the view of the mountains seemed even better, with the sun on the snow of the distant mountains. It was a friendly breakfast time, so we booked for coming back, in case it was busy over the bank holiday weekend. Off we went back to the busy motorway that took us over Beatock Summit and more snow, through Glasgow, and over the Clyde by the Erskine bridge - a long drive before lunch. Afterwards Chris got very tired and when she saw Loch Lomond she wanted to stop and find a place to stay looking over the loch. I stopped and took a photo of Ben Lomond in snow across the loch. "Not another snowy mountain", she said. I stopped at various possible places but they were no good. A couple of them didn't answer my knock. A lovely cottagey one had the bedroom upstairs and the loo downstairs - "No good", said Chris. One had far too many steps and another was full. It was a bit upsetting as I began to realise how disabled Chris was. But then we found it, off the main road, down a little drive, over a railway bridge, and there it was in a perfect setting amongst the hills around Crianlarich. We realised we had come north - it was cold, but the bedroom had fantastic views of snow-covered mountains both ways. It was like Switzerland, and the sun shone in and it was lovely and warm. The basket work chairs were most comfortable. I bought some food in the town to make our tea, and afterwards had a walk. The crocuses were out and the daffodils in tight bud! We were back to early spring - wonderful! It had been a long drive, and Chris was tired, but we were finished with motorways, and into the austere beauty of the Scottish mountains. How lucky we were to see them in snow, out of cloud, and in clear crisp sunshine. As the sun set, we watched the train on its way to Fort William and Mallaig, and heard the other half of the train passing near the house as it made its way to Oban and the Mull ferry. The next day there was no hurry. We chatted to the proprietor over our porridge and big cooked breakfast and admired the big trout caught in the nearby river by his son. We discovered he'd been to Ireland the year we had (1992) and been to Ballyferriter to play golf (we'd had our honeymoon there, and revisited it two years ago). It was very pleasant not to be rushing anywhere. So the car ambled along to Oban, with a leisurely stop for coffee, of course, and a view of the mouth of Loch Etive. The last time we'd come to Iona we'd had a boat trip up the loch. Oban was its usual busy self but so different from London. We went to the ferry terminal to get the tickets for the ferry and to book places on the ferries up to the Western Isles for later. We were so near to Iona now - surely nothing could stop us! We had a happy afternoon exploring the Bridge over the Atlantic, the Isle of Seil, and the Highland Arts Studio. There they plied us with shortbread and fudge, and we watched a video, and were tempted to buy presents and souvenirs. In the evening I walked down to the shore from the B&B we'd booked into, walked quite a distance and then sat to watch the sun set, over Mull. Chris was very tired and watched the TV news - John Curry had died of AIDS at 44.

Saturday was the day we crossed the sea to Iona. It is always exciting, going on a ferry, especially when you haven't been on one for a while. We had an earlyish breakfast, and then called at the shops for a film, and an alarm clock - our other one had broken. The ferry was fine, Chris managed the steps from the car deck and we looked out at the views, sipping coffee. The sea was like a mill pond, and the weather a bit cloudy but quite bright and clear. Then off we went on the single track road over Mull, with the car wheel still scraping and creaking a bit. Even Chris was excited enough to take a photo of snow capped Ben More. We stopped at Bunessan for a drink, and a photo of the memorial to Mary MacDonald who wrote 'Child in the Manger' set to the tune we know better for 'Morning has Broken'.

But Chris was getting agitated. She wanted to get to the ferry terminal at Fionnphort and get the luggage sorted out for the crossing. So after a bit of lunch we parked as near to the ferry as possible, and Chris began to sort, while I asked about times of ferries. We had a while to wait. Chris told me what there was to take: two large suitcases and several bags. I said, "Chris, how can we take all this. You know how unsteady you are, and I can't carry it all". I might as well have saved my breath. "Now I'm going to have a rest to get my strength up", she said, but she was looking very agitated. I could see her falling with that lot but it was no use arguing.

Then a coach driver came up. "Waiting for the ferry? There's one coming over now, especially for my party. They'll take you as well". I persuaded Chris to come - sitting there thinking about it was making her worse. I couldn't help her. We staggered down the road with our loads, me first to make sure the ferry waited for us. The sea was sloshing round the bottom of the ferry ramp - it was easy to get a shoeful. Chris was making a supreme effort, and then the ferryman was helping her. She collapsed on to a seat, and the ferry was off.

It had all happened so quickly - we just hoped we'd got all we wanted. It's a very short crossing, and we were there before we knew it. But there was no hurry the other end and we made our way slowly to the little tea place, where Chris sat down and I left her there to phone the abbey for transport. The van arrived, and as soon as they saw how Chris was, they helped me with the luggage and then helped her gently into the van. And from that moment the love and care of the Iona staff was all around us. With God's help we had arrived at our beloved Iona.

At Iona

Iona was very special to us. I had gone there with a group from my church in Birmingham after our last Sabbatical/Exchange to Oregon, USA. I had thought it would be a come-down after that, but it was not. Chris had not come that time. I was introduced to Celtic Spirituality, and to the pilgrimage round the island. It was then I began to understand pilgrimage as a symbolic journey, with meaningful stopping places saying different things. When Chris came with me it was General Election time, and we laughed as one member of the group - very left wing and concerned with justice and peace - pretended to be Mrs Thatcher, and a retired American Presbyterian minister pretended to be Ronald Reagan discussing on the telephone a proposal for an intercontinental ballistic missile site on Iona. A Czechoslovakian minister was deeply shocked that politicians should be mocked and laughed at! That time George MacLeod signed the papers for our postal vote, and we felt very honoured. He was there for the laying of the foundation stone of the new MacLeod Youth Centre. That time too, we were fortunate to have a beautiful day to go to the Island of Staffa with its hexagonal columns and its wonderful Fingals Cave. The boat had moored just at the entrance to the cave. One of the Americans asked, "Who built it?". And the answer was "The Good Lord". No wonder Mendelssohn was inspired to write music about such a fairy-tale place. Chris wanted it to be played at her funeral. Last time we were there we had heard Zaki Bedawi, a leading British Muslim, talk about Muslim Christian relations. That, too, had been a wonderful experience, with the call to prayer being heard in the Abbey cloisters and with him leading a worship service in the abbey.

So many famous people have been there. Our good American friend, who rang on the day of our send-off, still remembers meeting George MacLeod on Iona, many years ago. It is a story of resurrection, the rebuilding of the abbey by the clergy and the unemployed of Glasgow during the depression. There is an atmosphere which stems from the community started by St Columba so many years ago, when Iona, far from being isolated, was a great centre for the boat traffic up the West Coast of Scotland. Scottish Kings are buried there, and over the years a great peace and tranquillity has been built up in a very beautiful place. The worship at the abbey each day is well thought out and full of creativity, and participation involves young and old, and the volunteer staff. The abbey lends itself to worship which is innovatory, and there are services of great beauty and depth. The symbols of the wild goose and dove are to do with the Holy Spirit, and often an Atlantic gale will rattle the big door and blow around the Abbey, the wind invoking the spirit. The white doves flying round the abbey are reminders of St Columba, for Columba means dove. It is a place where the imagination is stimulated by the beauty of nature, the great variety of the people, the old stones of the Abbey and the ruined Nunnery, and the strange remnants of the Hermitage. The stone crosses stand in silent tribute as they have stood for hundreds and hundreds of years. Gerard Hughes, in his book recording his pilgrimage 'In Search of a Way' came to a desert island off Mull to be alone to help him concentrate on his prayers. It was windswept and cold, with a history that connected it to St Columba through his mother, and it was that book originally that made us think that we must go to Iona again.

We were driven up the road to the abbey in the blue van by a young Londoner - how far from London we felt! Cars are not allowed on the island without a special permit and anyway the total road length over the whole island can't be much more than two miles! All except the very frail walk up from the ferry, the van being used to take up the luggage. Marion (a Canadian) met us and she sorted our room out - next door to the bathroom and loos and close to the refectory. Steps with a good handrail led to the Cloisters, Abbey, and the conference room, and the common room with its lovely fire. Our bedroom had a efficient heater in it, so we were never cold, and a little window looked out over the sea to Mull. There was plenty of room to unpack. Off came the wig, and on went the headscarf. Cases and bags were emptied and put in drawers or hung up. Chris was happy - she had reached a goal and was relaxing. We went into the refectory to have a cup of tea and some home made chocolate cake. The volunteer chef produced some wonderful food for us during our stay. We were told of our chores: I joined the mop and bucket brigade, but Chris was excused because of her illness.

We met a doctor and his wife, whom we had met the last time with Zaki Bedawi. It was reassuring to know they were in the next room. One of Chris's eyes was very bloodshot, but the doctor didn't think it was of any great consequence, and gradually it went back to normal. Chris was rapidly making friends - a Polish girl called Jolanta and people from Wigtown Moor URC, Leeds. Chris was so good at catching on to who was who; I always got confused and relied on her to tell me. We went for a little walk to feel the cool invigorating wind around our faces, and make friends with the lambs. I went for a longer walk up to the North Shore, beloved of painters and photographers. The sky was cloudy, but the white sand was still bright to look at, and the islands around could be seen very clearly. Chris had two helpings of lasagne for the evening meal, and I had two helpings of pudding and cream! The abbey was cold for the evening service of welcome, but it was lovely. There was plenty of chatting before bed-time.

When I got up early on Sunday to go to the bathroom it was misty and very damp - not promising at all but I had forgotten how quickly it changes there. For the next time I looked the mist was rolling away and the sun was shining, heralding a really beautiful day - another day of resurrection.

We had heard how Easter Sunday at Iona had been very stormy and wet, with people not able to get across because the ferry couldn't operate. It was a disappointment for a lot of people. It was so right for us to have gone to Canterbury. At breakfast Chris was asked if she would help with the offering and the distribution at the Sunday abbey service. She was very pleased to be asked, and soon had to go down to rehearse. I went with her. The candles were lit and the sun was streaming in. I took my camera and got some very precious photos. Chris was standing by the attractive green and white Iona marble altar with the other helpers: little David, a lad from Wales wearing his baseball cap, Yolante from the USA, Hope, a Caribbean music teacher from a special project sponsored by the Council for World Mission in Wales, and Andrew. The sermon was preached by a Canadian woman minister on the Beatitudes using little anecdotes that were very moving. She also presided at the communion, while the warden of Iona (also a woman) led the liturgy. Chris wrote in her diary: "I leaned upon John Hull's 'rock', the marble altar, and asked for strength to be able to walk up that central aisle without faltering". She walked around taking up the offering. Then there was the procession down to the altar carrying the chalices and the bread (David carried the bread, still wearing his baseball cap!). After the institution and the prayers they came down the aisle. Chris was bearing a pottery chalice full of wine. There were steps and nothing to hold on to. I saw the doctor's amazed face. It was a demonstration of the power of God. She was held up by prayer. To me what I saw was unbelievable - the power of the Holy Spirit. She bore in the chalice a symbol of the life of God, but she herself was also a symbol of that life and power. Back she went to the altar for the concluding prayers, and back up the aisle in procession with Hope to take the chalices back to the vestry. I will never forget that service, and the photos I took of her taking part in the rehearsal are very special.

This is what Chris wrote in a letter to friends at Birmingham -

"One of my challenges at the Abbey was being asked to help distribute the wine in heavy chalices and take up the offertory (also heavy!). I had to walk the length of the aisle, negotiate steps, and stand for some time behind the marble altar! I managed it, drawing strength from those ancient stones, and the Healing and Peace we have always found there! John said it was a miracle - and he was working out the cost if I fell and smashed the pottery chalice! It was a very woman-oriented service led by the Warden (a woman), the President and Preacher, a young Canadian woman minister, and served by three of us and a young man. One was a Jamaican girl, over here with CWM, who knows Francis Brienen, the Dutch Training in Mission student we had at St Columba, Moseley. She is on a project in South Wales at present (the children with her helped in one of the services, and one of the lads wearing a baseball cap, carried up the bread)".

The sun shone strongly out of a deep blue sky (just as it had at Canterbury at Easter) and we sat outside for coffee out of the wind and in the sun, looking at the vivid dark blue sea and snow capped Ben More on Mull. After lunch (it seemed right to be lamb - there is a lamb with a cross carved on the font in the abbey) we walked down to the nunnery. Chris sat on a seat in the sun while I went off to Martyr's Bay and took photos of sheep, white sand, blue sea, and the mountains of Mull. When I got back she was still knitting the little white jacket for Sue's baby, and wondering how she was going to get back to the abbey, it seemed to be such a long way. It was only about 100 yards, I think - maybe a little more - but she had used up all her strength at the service. We looked in at the plain Church of Scotland church on the way to give her a rest.

There was another fairly hilarious getting to know you session, with some songs too, and then there was silent worship in the abbey but not too silent as there were a lot of children and young people. I got to know two students at Spurgeons in South Norwood, and a vicar having a sabbatical getting over 'burn out'. It had been an unforgettable day.

The next day was cloudy. Chris had had a very wakeful night so I reduced her steroid dose as per the consultant's instructions. Cwti, one of the leading members of staff, did a session on the history of Iona and Columba. Though we knew a lot, she was quite brilliant, and seems to live perpetually on overdrive - quick, witty, but a deep thinker too. Chris was very tired, so she stayed in writing letters and postcards, one of which has since been given back to me as a memento. On it Chris says: "This is a healing place". I walked up to the top of Dun I (the highest point) and over to the other side of the island to the machair (a green grassy place made of tiny shells) and to St Columba's bay where the saint landed so long ago. I threw a stone in the sea as one should (to get rid of guilt) and picked up two others as souvenirs. It rained a bit, and I got a little wet, but it wasn't too bad.

The evening service was arranged by the cook, David, from Portland, Oregon (it's a small world), with help from the kids. I have never seen anything like it. The Abbey guide was crouching on the stone floor in a thin teeshirt, surrounded by nightlights. It was very dark. Part of the letter of James was read, about the evil potential of the tongue, then there were the insults - 'Homo', 'Nigger', 'Piece of Shit', 'Cow', 'Dirty old man' fifteen of them in all, and each time he flinched and put a nightlight out. Then came the questions, "Who are you?" and as he answered the nightlights were re-lit. "I am forgiven", "I am a person", "I am loved by God", "God created me". It was shocking, yet full of meaning, and though the young people no doubt had fun thinking up the insults, they saw the point of it. Iona is full of surprises at worship.

Chris was a little sad that we would not be there the next evening, the weekly healing service. But her new friends asked if she would like her name to be mentioned there, and she was very pleased to be thought about at this wonderful place. But our pillar of cloud was moving on.

I have always found Iona to be a place that draws you, and then pushes you away. We had been greatly inspired, even in such a short time. Now it was raining and windy. We chatted away and made yet more friends and then we packed up regretfully, but we still had a long way to go. It was our last night in Iona together.

We slept well and woke to lovely sunshine. We had breakfast with the doctor and his wife. I had two bowls of porridge! The morning prayers finished with 'You shall go out with joy' and 'the trees of the field shall clap their hands'. We put some threads of wool on the prayer net - what a lovely idea - a change from lighting candles. People were all giving us good wishes and saying they would pray for us, and after chores and a coffee we were off in the van, with Cwti coming with us - that was lovely of her. We came to Iona for inspiration, and we found it. We also found the loving care of a Christian community - everyone surrounding us with prayer and concern. It is the place of the comforter, the strengthener, as well as the inspirer; the place of visions, and the place of the power of God, the power of love and a healing place: the wind, the dove, the wild goose, the Holy Spirit, God in action. At Iona we found the faith and inspiration to go on to the end of the pilgrimage. We needed Iona to do that, and it didn't fail us. As the secret garden showed us resurrection and prepared us for Easter, so Iona showed us the Holy Spirit and prepared us for Pentecost. It was another piece of the jigsaw in place.

Further North

Cwti helped us with our bags onto the ferry - so different from getting on at the other side. As it started off the rain poured down - but she was still waving to us. We sat in the little covered area and watched Iona receding - pilgrims on the move again- the next goal not far away. The zip on one of the cases had broken and I hoped it would hold together till we got to the car. Its contents were bulging out! We staggered off the ferry: the car seemed to be waiting patiently for us and we packed everything in. We had a quick stop at Bunessan to post yet more letters and cards, and then we were off on the road we had come along, but instead of getting the big ferry back to Oban, we went round the island to Fishnish to get the little ferry to Lochaline. I had hoped there'd be a cafe somewhere, but no, not a sign of one. We got to the ferry point at Fishnish - totally desolate, but there was a little burger bar and a lady in it, cooking. It was a complete surprise and one we needed as we were pretty hungry. We had a cup of tea while she cooked, then carried the burgers in paper to the car to eat them. Chris dropped hers - "Oh well, they're clean stones", she said, scraping it up. Then I did the same and we both laughed. We munched away happily, waiting for the ferry which arrived on time. It was a little ferry, so we stayed in the car - there was no real deck to get out on to.

After a very necessary stop at Lochaline (another pretty desolate place) there was a very long drive along single track roads to Mallaig. Chris went out like a light! I'm quite happy driving along with no one talking, and I concentrated on the route, which was very twisty and hilly. There were only one or two junctions, and each time I carefully consulted the map for a wrong turn could have landed us many miles out of our way. The car was behaving quite well, even though the noise on the wheel hadn't gone away, and I seemed to be crashing the gears a bit. Eventually we got to Arisaig and I spotted a tea place and parked. Chris woke up and asked what she'd missed and I regaled her with hills, lochs and even a wildcat! She was pleased about the cafe tea, scones and rolls with a lovely view across the sea and I was pleased to get over that stretch - very desolate and lonely, hardly any traffic, not the place to break down, no garages for petrol. Fortunately I'd filled up the tank completely at Oban.

So now it wasn't far to Mallaig - we'd been this way before - wonderful views of Rhum and Eigg, white sand, photogenic if only I could have stopped. We went straight to the ferry terminal to book the tickets for Skye, and then I went to the garage for petrol. Quite suddenly the gears were worse. I couldn't get into first without crashing it. Unfortunately the garage didn't do repairs. "There's one at Morar down the road. If you hurry they might still be open". And they were. The man watched me trying to change gear and said, "The clutch cable needs adjusting - I'm not sure if it will". He looked, and said, "It's your lucky day. Going to Skye, are you? It's not much fun breaking down there. There you are - try it now". It was so much better - and he refused payment. "I'll charge it up to the AA", he said, taking my membership number. He checked the wheel too, and pronounced it okay.

We found a nice little B&B just by the ferry, and a cafe where it was chips with everything. I ate my jumbo sausage, and Chris her chicken piece, to the strains of Danny Boy (amongst other things). That song always took us back to a little pub in South West Ireland where it was sung by a girl with a lovely voice. That was on our honeymoon. It was a lovely end to a rather fraught day - well, not quite the end. I went off for a walk to see the sunset and Chris sat on the quay for a while watching the boats. A ferry terminal is always fascinating. The last time we'd left Mallaig we'd chased a steam train in the car - road and rail are side by side - the last steam train on BR - or rather Scot Rail.

The next morning we had plenty of time before the ferry and we had ordered a 9 o'clock breakfast. We ate it in a leisurely fashion, watching the boats from the window. It was a beautiful sunny morning and we made the most of the bank and the post office as we didn't know when we'd see such things again, and then we were off into the wilds. The crossing was very calm with views of the Cuillins, Rhum and Eigg - superb. Then we were off on the single track road across Skye. I hoped we'd have time to take the scenic route from Portree round the coast to Uig, the next ferry place. It was a bit cloudy now and I took one or two photos though it was not really very scenic. After a photo stop, I got in and drove off from the lay-by, put my foot on the clutch to go into second gear, there was a 'ping' and the pedal seemed to disappear. We stopped. I look at Chris. "That's the clutch cable broken", I said. "Is it serious?" she asked. "Well, I can't move", I said, "I can't even get it back into the lay-by". We sat there wondering what to do. I remembered the garage man's remarks about breaking down in Skye. I think Chris felt that that was the end of our journey and we'd not get to Ian and Linda's after all, but I felt that now we were on Skye Ian would come and fetch us, if the worst came to the worst.

Along came a car and stopped. It was going in the opposite direction to us. He had to stop - there was no way round. He helped me push the car back into the lay-by. "And now what are you going to do?" he said cheerily. I said something about a telephone - that was a joke - this was hardly the Ml! Country living is so different. He was wonderful. It appears we were only 4 miles from a really modern garage so he took us there and waited while they contacted the AA for me. It didn't seem long before they'd fetched the car and confirmed my verdict. There was one snag - they hadn't a clutch cable for my car. They thought there might be one in Portree, but they'd have to wait till after lunch to phone them.

The garage had a lounge, and a shop that sold food and drinks - very civilised. We just had to be patient. We both realised just how helpless Chris was without a car, but eventually it was established that Portree had what we wanted, and could send it on the school bus! More waiting. At least I could walk around and see the place - it was beautiful - Chris found it very annoying that the lounge was upstairs and the loo downstairs, but she coped. The school bus came at 4.30 and off got a schoolboy with a parcel, my clutch cable. Chris and I went off to a candle-maker by the sea and bought some souvenirs, and when we got back the car was ready. We had been so lucky - or was it luck? We could have been 20 or 30 miles from that garage. We could have been on that wild road from Lochaline yesterday. We thanked God - we felt the power of the prayers of so many people. We ate fish and chips at Portree, and then drove on to Uig. It was sheeting down, and blowing a gale. "It's been like this all day", said our landlady at the B&B, though we'd had dry sunny weather at the garage. It had been another fraught day and Chris was tired and anxious. This part of the journey was turning out to be a bit of a battle. I 'phoned Ian and Linda - they were expecting us for lunch the next day. As we sat in the bedroom having our cocoa, there were bangs outside. It was a sheet on the line, the wind trying to tear it apart, the rain still pouring down. You had to be tough to live up here. The bangs went on all night!

The next morning we woke to heavy snow, with the hills (when you could see them) quite white, but the breakfast was really good - lots of everything. We tucked into sausage, egg, bacon, fried bread - two of everything - lots of toast, cereals and tea. We needed it all to keep warm, and Chris looked apprehensive in the warmest clothes she had. It looked as if the ferry ride would be rough - two hours at sea this time out into the Atlantic.

It was a good thing I'd booked at Oban as the ferry was full. But we had to wait after I'd produced the return tickets because the ferry was a bit late. The snow fell and I kept the engine running to keep the car warm. Eventually we were on. Chris looked at the steps and said, "No, I can't get up there", so we got the men to take us up in the lift - no trouble at all. Wherever we were we found nothing but kindness and consideration.

Chris was worried. She'd seen some people taking sea-sickness pills. She sat in the cafeteria with her head down most of the time, sipping coffee and eating shortbread biscuits. She didn't look well, but there was nothing I could do to help, so after a while I went out on deck and there was rewarded with a most wonderful view. We were coming out of the snow and the cloud. Uig had disappeared from sight and there was Harris in sunshine, covered in snow. It was a glorious panorama - I felt I was arriving in Iceland or Greenland and my camera was in the car in the locked car deck! But it would have been difficult to photograph to get the effect. I shall always remember it, standing in a cold gale of wind under heavy cloud, with that bright snowy horizon coming slowly nearer. It was too cold to stand there for long, but I kept looking out, as did a man with a video camera trying to capture it. No-one else came up to see and I knew Chris's attitude to snow, and how she was feeling anyway. I suddenly felt confident again. We were winning through - we were getting to our goal. Eventually we got out of the open sea and into the channel leading to Tarbert, and everything was green. The snow I had seen was on the mountains, and that's all that could be seen from far away.

I went to tell Chris we weren't far away. She was looking much better and looking out at the new island we had arrived at - Harris - and appreciating the sunshine after snowy Uig.

Soon we were driving away from the ferry into the snowy mountains above the snow line on a winding single track road with roadworks. When you came to the roadworks you had to leave the road and drive on the bare mountain! We hoped it was the road! It didn't say 'Stornoway' but something a bit like it which we assumed was the Gaelic spelling. We were in a different world, barren, peaty, with a few houses now and again. After the mountains of Harris, Lewis was flatter but desolate and mostly brown. Then we saw the junction where we turned left - right in the middle of the peaty wilderness. It took us towards the West coast and suddenly Chris said, "There are the stones!". They looked so small, and near to some buildings, not a bit like I had imagined, but of course we were some way away. But there was the name on the road sign - Callanish. We had arrived at another of Chris's goals. We got a bit lost, going too far looking for a garage which we thought would look like ones with petrol pumps! Soon we were at Ian and Linda's. There was Ian, 3 stone heavier than we'd last seen him, Linda just as we remembered her, and Rachel 2 and a half and Anne 7 months. Then we were sitting down to a meal in their very spacious house, making friends with the children, and looking out at the view over the loch. It was a bright sunny day. Suddenly we could relax after our battle up north to get here. We were as far away from Sedlescombe as South Norway, Berlin, Venice, or Barcelona.

Callanish

We weren't actually at Callanish, but it's easier to say and spell than Tolsta Chaolais (pronounced Tolshta Choolish with the Ch as in loch)! But Callanish was just a mile or two down the road.

We had three totally independent connections with Callanish. First was the book by William Horwood about the golden eagle from London Zoo, his Duncton books also feature stones and their special powers. No doubt he visited Callanish at one time and his book *'Stonor Eagles'* is partly based in Skye not so far away. Both Chris and I had read the book *'Callanish'* sometime earlier.

Then there was the poster. Chris, as a result of her CEM connections, received RE Today, a quarterly magazine, and kept up her interest after leaving Birmingham. The poster is actually in the Autumn 1992 magazine, so Chris would have read it a little before she sat on that seat in the garden house at Sayers Common writing her prayer. It's a tear out poster from the middle of the magazine, so on the back are the notes for a school project about stones, written by the CEM secretary for Scotland. It says: "Stones have a mystery about them, they have a sense of timelessness about them, they are an expression of the inexpressible. Stones are used to signify God or places of worship. Standing stones bear witness to vanished cultures".

Lastly there was Ian and Linda, though I don't think we connected them with Callanish until Ian sent the Evening Primrose Oil capsules when he heard Chris was to have radiotherapy, and we saw the word Callanish on the bottle because the factory is there.

I'm also not sure when we put the three connections together, but it is an unusual name and one would remind us of the others quite quickly, I suppose.

Ian and Linda had been asking us to visit for a long time, and we had always dismissed it as too far. Our son, Tim, has had a few free holidays with them, but at first they didn't live near Callanish, although Ian worked there. Tim wasn't interested in standing stones anyway, much more keen on the hills, the sea and photography.

We really discussed going only during our thoughts about the pilgrimage. I had always been fascinated to go and see what the Outer Hebrides, or Western Isles, were like, but I think Chris only agreed to go because of the stones, the poster, and the theme of freedom in the book. It was always a bit of an optional extra to Iona for a long time, but then it became a challenge for both of us - the furthest point to be attained. Then it became a fascination as we looked at the poster, put up in the cottage, sharing the same place of honour as the one from Turvey Abbey *'He is Risen'*.

Of course, there was always the link with the Evening Primrose Oil which Chris took regularly for about a year, continuing right up to her death. It was important for her to take it, and it is likely it had beneficial effects in several ways, particularly protecting her from radiation burns. In the same way it was important for her to get to the stones, for they were one of her goals. Though they have no specifically religious significance, it is what they symbolised to Chris that was important, and one of these things was freedom, and linked up with her reading of *'Cancer Ward'*. Chris's spirituality has always been a bit linked up with superstition; she hated owls, for instance, linking them with death. So the idea of a presence or power linked up with a group of stones would not be difficult for her to go along with in an imaginative way. But it was partly in fun - she was curious to see them, they gave her a goal to aim for, and it was lovely to accept Ian and Linda's offer to have us for we thought a lot of each other.

Ian had suggested that Chris might consider being a guinea-pig for testing a derivative of the Evening Primrose Oil given in very large amounts. There was evidence it might have helped to kill off the cancer cells. It would have needed hospitalisation, or at least an intensive course of treatment through the hospital. Like the prayers for healing, Chris politely turned the idea down, and Ian wasn't upset about it. It had only been a suggestion. The curious way in which Callanish came up from three directions makes one wonder if, like some of the other things in the pilgrimage, it was meant to be. And if so, why? I'll come back to that question after I've talked about some of the things that happened during our week's stay.

Life on Lewis

We arrived on Primrose Day, April 21st, as Chris mentions in her diary. We had left primroses in our cottage garden, and we saw them flowering everywhere we went. Even on barren windswept Lewis we found a little sheltered bank with some in flower. After we arrived and had lunch, Ian and I and the children set out to explore the village, while Chris and Linda chatted and unpacked. We have always got on well with them. For several years they ran the Cubs and Scouts at Moseley for me, very efficiently and the work prospered greatly under their leadership. They were also part of a successful 20s-30s group meeting on Sundays at our house, and have kept up friendships made there ever since, as have we, but Tim was the one who really kept in touch after they moved to Lewis. He was able to go up during holidays from the Missions to Seamen and they provided a car for him to roam around Lewis and Harris. Both Ian and Linda are Scottish, and when the job was offered, they were thrilled to go from Oxford, where Ian was then doing research. Most people would not have been so thrilled, but for Ian and Linda, loving the open air life, and capable of doing 40 mile walks together, it was a challenge not to be missed.

We heard from Tim that they were building their own house and going into a kind of crofting life style, with peat fires. In fact our image of the house was quite wrong. It was a new building, timber framed clad with concrete of some type, with a large layer of insulation to keep in the heat, and a modern boiler that runs on peat, but also oil fired central heating! Ian explained that a brick built house would not stand up to the winds, it would crack, but timber bends and stands up to the Atlantic gales better. He said that the winter before last they had had 4 months of continuous gales, and had learnt to walk bent double to stop being blown over. This accounts for the treeless landscapes.

He told me the village of Tolsta Chaolais is Viking in origin, built around the little loch which has a narrow outlet into the sea at high tide. Until relatively recently the people lived in Black Houses, stone buildings with a thatched roof held down against the wind by ropes and heavy stones. These have been abandoned now in favour of new technology, and very few survive. The roofs were taken off so that they didn't have to pay rates on them. Ian showed me the old field system, now largely abandoned, but built up over centuries of cultivation and abandoned in the Scottish clearances. He said it is almost impossible to reclaim it now, destroyed by neglect. As we walked by the few houses that made up the village, we heard noises of machinery coming from little wooden huts with tin roofs. Ian explained they were hand looms, making the famous Harris Tweed cloth. People sign an agreement not to use powered machinery. It is operated by a treadle and apart from sheep and the Callanish factory is really the only industry. There are no shops in the village, the nearest ones being at Stornoway 25 miles away. We walked along the road with no cars, the sheep and hens roaming free, children playing, piles of peat by the houses, and the little wooden huts with the sound of looms working, and it was like going back in time, but not quite. The houses were pretty new, there were cars by the houses, and the road was in good repair. The village was full of folk like Ian and Linda determined to make a go of it in this desolate area - people who were prepared to do battle with the harsh conditions because they liked the lifestyle.

In the summer they go peat-cutting together and they help one another out in many ways. Ian rang up a sheep owner when he got back to tell him how we had seen a tiny lamb near the road, separated from its mother, and likely to perish if something wasn't done quickly. It was just so far removed from the life we know, even in Sedlescombe. On this particular day the sun was out and it wasn't really cold and it was beautiful. "It's a pity you weren't a bit later", said Ian, "the wild flowers come out everywhere, and it looks really lovely". Spring hadn't really started there! But in the shelter of the porchway there were some hyacinths out. Ian picked some and put them in our bedroom - the scent was almost overpowering. What a lovely thought. Chris had got out presents she had brought for the children, little dolls and crayons from the Isle of Seil near Oban, and a story book about Mull which she had bought on the ferry, with pictures in it to colour. It started off: "in Mull either it is raining, or has just rained, or is about to rain!" We decided Lewis is very similar. The children stayed up very late and Linda looked pretty tired. We gradually discovered that Rachel and Anna were both pretty well tireless, day and night, wearing poor Mum out. Anna was nearly walking despite her age (Rachel walked at 8 months) and only seemed happy when someone took her by the hand and she walked along - very wearing and not too good for the back! But it was good to be surrounded by young life, and we thought of Matthew, and Sue less than a month away from giving birth.

The next day was sunny and quite calm and I decided to go to the Butt of Lewis lighthouse of Shipping Forecast fame, and Chris decided to come in spite of saying she wouldn't earlier on. We went through a sleet shower (of course). What a fantastic place - sheer high cliffs, wild sea - even that day. 50 miles away we saw the Scottish mainland near Cape Wrath, snow-covered. What a wonderful view! And there was a coffee shop, run by a Yorkshire couple from Holmfirth, dependent on coach trips for custom, I dare say.

We went to the Callanish Evening Primrose Oil factory in the afternoon for a tour round. It had been a fish drying factory, but was taken over by Scotia Holdings for the distillation and purification of the oil from the Evening Primrose - which is grown in fields in Writtle near Colchester. Ian gave us a talk about it in a room where there was an intriguing painting - a combination of the factory, the standing stones, a research worker and his chemical equipment, and a clump of evening primroses. He told us of gama-linolenic acid, the active ingredient of the drug, which is used by the body to produce compounds that are anti-inflammatory. He talked of its use with eczema, diabetes, cancer and AIDS. We told him of Chris's cousin Geoff in Market Rasen who takes it for multiple sclerosis. Ian was so enthusiastic we could see he really believed in the importance of his work for medicine, and we believed it was helping Chris's condition. It was good to be there.

We went to Stornoway the next day - only 25 miles to the nearest shop! It's a busy place and there are only a few trees. We saw the ferry that goes to Ullapool and were glad we didn't plan to go back that way - a 4 hour crossing, often very rough - two hours was bad enough for Chris. We bought souvenirs. I took a photo of Chris at the harbour to show she had got there. We patronised a Cancer Research sale and were glad to be able to do it. We got wet in the rain now and then! As we came back we passed the stones, and I drove up to them. It was raining and they were quite dramatic in silhouette against the grey sky and the loch. I took some photos and we went back to Ian and Linda's. Later I went back to the stones to catch them in the evening sun but it just went in as I got there, so the next morning we tried again, and both got some photos. I took Chris leaning against one of them - was she gaining strength from the stones as she did from the marble altar at Iona? They are very ancient - going back nearly 4,000 years. We learnt that they were orientated to the moon rather than the sun - different from Stonehenge. There are over 50 stones with a circle, an avenue and a burial chamber. In fact, their spatial configuration, if you looked at them from the air, is a bit like an enormous Iona cross. We stayed there for a while thinking our own thoughts. We had come to one of Chris's goals. We tried to remember the poster in the cottage kitchen and wondered which stones there were on that. There are so many it is difficult to take a photo to give a general impression, but they are very photogenic with the different configurations and constantly changing light. It was a strange experience, searching for meanings. Had God brought us there? Why? Everything seemed shrouded in mystery - the mystery of a bygone age. We would never come here again together. There was a skylark singing. It was a Sunday and we were at these ancient stones instead of at worship. We didn't feel close to God, nor any really special atmosphere, and we didn't stay long.

After a happy day with Ian and Linda, we decided to go to the Wee Frees Kirk. The service was in English only in the evening. It was raining hard, yet the car park was full, and the church likewise. It was very plain both inside and out. Metrical psalms were sung seated, with a precentor starting each verse. There was no accompaniment. The readings were psalms, too. We stood for the prayers, which were long and elaborate. The sermon was about the psalms, also, and went on and on, again elaborate but not inspiring to Chris or me. Everyone suddenly stood up as he said "Amen" at the end, as if he had given an order. At the end of the service everyone filed out in order, beginning at the back. Chris felt dizzy and had to lean on me to go out in turn. There was no fellowship afterwards, and no real welcome at the beginning. We were neither of us inspired. There was no joy, no enthusiasm, no gospel. I felt sorry for Ian and Linda, having to live in a place with a church like this, but they were there with a lovely roast beef dinner to warm and cheer us up. It had been a strange Sunday.

In fact Ian wrote to me later that the Lewis folk are very friendly, warmhearted and welcoming, and full of fun. It is only their style of worship that is strange.

On Monday it was a lovely day and we went on a scenic tour down the West side of the island, meeting a disabled man from Sheffield enjoying being away from it all. At one point I left Chris in the car ready for a sleep while I went off up a hill to take some photos. On the way back I lost the path, and found myself in a very steep place where one slip could have been very dangerous. I inched my way slowly across to safer ground and told myself I had been a fool. Chris was so dependent on me now so what was I doing putting myself quite unnecessarily in danger? When I got back she was awake and blissfully unaware of my stupidity. I did not tell her but felt the isolation of this place - beautiful scenery, but stark, harsh and unforgiving. I began to feel it was time to start our way home. Chris's strength was failing and we needed to be in gentler places, so we had another day in Stornoway buying gifts, and shopping for Linda while it rained and blew a gale. Chris said the wind was 'wuthering around' and even the natives admitted it was a bit blustery, but it was a good day, and I managed to phone and make arrangements for our journey south! When we got back Ian showed us things he had got through the post to help grow plants in the garden and protect them from the wind. Later we learnt that all his efforts had blown away in a gale! We gave them our gift, a chrysanthemum for <u>inside</u> the house, and then they gave us theirs - two little framed paintings, one of the stones, and an illustrated map of the island by a local artist. Ian had brought, also, lots of evening primrose oil from the factory, and some multivitamins too - all labelled Callanish. We felt their love and generosity towards us in this cold and harsh place, and were very grateful.

I think I know, now, why God brought us there. All those people living in that village are prepared to take up the challenge and battle against the elements to make a livelihood. Life is a battle, but it's worth it, and they care for each other and learn to love the life. There are many blessings to be had that cannot be found elsewhere.

In the same way Chris and I were facing a battle, not against the elements, but against Chris's increasing weakness Seeing Ian believing in what he was doing, and Linda tired but determined to make a loving home for her children, I was proud to know them both, and they inspired me to battle on to make Chris's last months full and meaningful. It would be hard, but it would be worth it. I felt toughened up by the cold and wet, the wind and sun, and the durability of the standing stones, standing against 4,000 years of wind, rain and snow.

> *"I shall not fear the battle, if thou art by my side*
> *Nor wander from the pathway, if thou wilt be my guide"*

With God, we should win through and find many blessings yet, that perhaps we could only find by going through the battles ahead. The Holy Spirit is like the wind, it blew through the room where the disciples were, and the flames sat on each of their heads, blessing each one. This is Pentecost, frightening, aweful, yet beautiful and loving.

The Journey Back

The ferry back to Skye was late in the day, so there was no rush to leave. We said goodbye to Ian as he went to work. Ian and Chris must have realised it was the last time. We had a happy time relaxing with the children in the morning but eventually it was time to go. There were hugs and kisses all round. We'd had a lovely time - quite unforgettable - and we made our way down the single track road across the desolate landscape. We went past the 'wee frees' and the stones. There was a place where we could see three stone circles at once. Why was the place so important to the stone circle builders thousands of years ago? We had decided to stop at a shop somewhere, or a cafe, to pick up a bit of food although we'd been very well fed and didn't need much. We'd been there a week and we'd forgotten there were no shops or cafes.

We approached the mountains of Harris, now having lost their snow and looking quite different. At the last village before the ascent there was a shop just about to close, and I bought some bits for lunch. We stopped by the roadside, eating and looking at the view. A very occasional vehicle passed, yet it is the only road from Stornoway to Tarbert, the main towns. I remembered the A road by Ian's, where I was walking the night before, and where I shooed a lamb off the road because I heard a car - it had fallen asleep curled up in the middle of the road! I tried to imagine the M25 and couldn't!

Eventually we got to Tarbert, very early for the ferry, and went to the Harris Hotel for coffee. There were trees and soft greens in this sheltered spot, and we relaxed feeling we were coming to civilisation again. Chris copied a poem that was up on the wall - here's a bit of it:

'I met a man in Harris Tweed as I walked down the Strand.
I turned and followed him like a dog
The breath of hill and sea and bog
That clung about that coat of brown.
And suddenly in London Town
I heard again the Gaelic speech
The sound of keel on shingly beach;
The traffic's never ending roar
Came plangent from a shining shore,
I saw the little lochs where lie
The lilies white as ivory
And tumbling down the rocky hills
Came scores of little foaming rills......

I had a Harris Tweed jacket bought in Margate but with the label 'Hand woven in the Outer Hebrides'. The memories would come to us in London too.

For us it was more than a holiday or a visit. We were driven by the wind of the Spirit to make a journey full of symbolic meaning. It was an achievement that had seemed impossible. We had climbed the hill of 'Difficulty' (as Christian had in *Pilgrim's Progress*).

Chris put her head down on the table on the ferry as the swell began to rock us up and down, but the crossing was better than we'd feared and at Uig our bed and breakfast lady was welcoming and waiting to hear our story. The sheet still flapped on the line, but the snow was gone. The next day we sped across Skye full of mist and cloud and sudden views of the black Cuillin mountains. A Yorkshire lady gave us coffee, full of grumbles about the tourists who stole things from her, and thought her prices too high. We were back in civilisation. We waved at the garage that had been so good on our way up. At Kyle of Lochalsh we were off the island

and onto the mainland before Chris realised we'd set off! On and on we went on a fast road, so different from the single track ones we'd been used to, past beautiful views of lochs and castles that seemed so tame and touristy, and there were cafes for a lunch stop - we had a choice! We ordered, and Chris went off to the loo. She was away some time, but that was not too unusual. Eventually the waitress arrived with the meal, and I asked if she'd mind seeing if Chris was all right. She'd got locked in the disabled loo (she always used them now, if there was one) - not enough strength to turn the handle. She was annoyed with herself. She'd be glad to get back home now.

On past lines of snow covered peaks, through Glencoe, black and threatening, the rain pouring down in great cascades, over the top to stop with the lorry drivers for a large cup of tea from a mobile cafe. Still it poured till we came to our B&B at Crianlarich again, where there was a wonderful rainbow across the view we had seen as we came up - then snow covered peaks in cold crisp air - now cloud, mist and rain, and shafts of sunlight.

We went on again the next day past misty Loch Lomond, the mountains hidden, and into busy Glasgow, racing past offices and tenements and factories, then on and on over the hills again to Carlisle and England at last. Chris slept and I drove. The view was hazy - we had forgotten what haze was. Soon we were in Pooley Bridge, busy for the Bank holiday - a good thing we'd booked. It was all so different. There were leaves on the trees and the hills were misty with no snow, the breeze felt warm, the gardens were beautiful with flowers and people were putting up tents and siting caravans. We awarded ourselves cream teas and rang Tim to wish him a happy birthday, and talked to the people at our B&B about our adventures.

Next day we drove on again past Liverpool, Walsall and Birmingham, where we had had churches over the years, to Coventry, my birth-place, to stay with Joyce and Robert, our 'in-laws' (parents of Dave's wife, Ruth). They gave us a lovely welcome and we talked of our adventures, and of our respective families. Chris was pretty shattered, and refused the offer of a shower the next morning - most unusual, but she was tired and unsteady. She did, however, want to go to Coventry Cathedral for the Sunday service and God had a pilgrimage surprise arranged for us!

Chris had been disappointed the previous Sunday that there was nothing on the radio about the women's ordinations at Coventry, but at the Cathedral this day, the preacher was Revd Sue Hardwick, cathedral chaplain, who spoke about her feelings at her ordination the week before. She talked about the realisation of her dreams as she had come in with the procession, looking at the great tapestry of Christ throned in majesty, and how she had gone out looking through the great John Piper window onto the old cathedral and the world outside. We felt her excitement. Chris had got herself involved with the wonderful feelings of the women looking forward to their ordinations in Southwark Cathedral. Sue Hardwick linked it in a interesting way with the thrill of the 102 year old woman in South Africa who was going to vote, and with Bishop Tutu dancing and people saying: "Today is the realisation of our dreams." "Dreams are important," she said, "they are horizons of possibilities." She quoted *Psalm 32* 'I shall instruct you and teach you the way to go. I shall not take my eyes off you'. God had allowed us to realise our dreams of the pilgrimage too. It all fitted to make it an inspiring occasion for us - and it was so unexpected.

But there was more. Chris had nudged me at the beginning of the service and pointed out on the service sheet that the celebrant was someone she knew, and as we came to the sharing of the peace, a lady came over to me, and as she shared she said, "I know you, don't I?" I said, "You're Rosemary, aren't you?" "Yes", she said, "Is Chris here?" She hadn't recognised her. The steroids were taking their toll, and her features were changing, and it had been a long time. They had been colleagues 10 years before, working for the Christian Education Movement.

After the service there was a long talk between them, and the celebrant, Rosemary's husband now, came over too. It was a wonderful, unplanned occasion which God must have planned for us. There were all the links - the CEM posters of Turvey Abbey's 'The Risen Christ', and of the Callanish Stones; the women's ordinations that were happening and would finish up our pilgrimage on the Eve of Pentecost in Southwark Cathedral; freedom in South Africa and Chris's search for freedom following her reading of Solzenitzin's *'Cancer Ward'*.

In the service they had prayed for Warwick Road URC where I had been baptised and Dave and Ruth had met. I went into the Chapel of Unity where they had a German/English Advent service, and where we had taken the 20s-30s group with the German au pairs, including Ina, whose wedding we hoped to attend in October - the same group Ian and Linda had belonged to. It was such a lovely time; like a lot of things on this pilgrimage it was meant. The pillar of cloud had led us.

And the day contained another lovely visit. After a splendid lunch given us by Robert and Joyce, we drove to Uxbridge to see Sue and Simon, and our lively grandchild, Matthew. We gave out presents from Scotland. He wasn't bothered with the steering wheel and the hat so much as the little bag of soap. He carried it round with him all afternoon. Sue, very pregnant now, and Simon proudly showed us round their beautiful new house and garden and we were very thrilled for them. We sat outside for tea - it was quite warm enough - back in the South again, and we drove across London in the evening arriving in East Dulwich at 9 o'clock. Chris wrote in her diary: "Lovely to be back! We made our challenge. Thank you Lord".

Three weeks to Pentecost

The first three days after our return it was a question of sorting out two overgrown gardens, going through the post, looking at our photos of the pilgrimage, doing all the washing, chatting with the neighbours, and getting up to date with what was happening at the church. I had a day at the cottage on my own to catch up with things there. It was a busy time but we got through it well. Chris was on form, very determined to get on with things so that the Dulwich house would be ready to come back to at the end of the Sabbatical. She went round the house dusting, hoovering, watering the plants, and went outside with the washing, admiring the lovely spring garden just about at its best with lilac, laburnum and apple blossom, aubretia, bluebells and tulips. She was so annoyed when the snooker final put *'Cry Freedom'* an hour late starting. We watched the film to the end (the early hours) and Chris found it exciting and important, and made me excited too!

Then we moved back down to the cottage for our last nine days there. After Dulwich, it was most restful, and we got into reading. Both of us were reading George McDonald, fairy stories for me, which I had bought in Stornoway, and for Chris *'The Curate's Awakening'* which I had bought her for Easter. She really got into it, and it became an important book for her. It's about a curate who drifted from university into the church without thinking much about it. His uncle had left him a legacy of lots of his sermons for each week of the year, so he just read those to his congregation on Sundays and everyone was happy until one day, a man who only came to church because he was keen on a girl there said to him: "You don't really believe all that stuff you preach do you?". So begins the curate's questioning of what he himself did believe, helped by a deformed man who was very ugly and handicapped, but spiritually very deep thinking. Then the curate has to deal with a very difficult pastoral problem. The girl's brother has come home talking about having committed murder, and the girl is sheltering him and hiding him away, though the brother wants to confess. Finally the brother dies (he was suffering from mental and physical illness) but has been able to offload his burden of guilt and accept forgiveness. The girl is distraught, wondering where her brother is, now he is dead, and the end of the book is about belief in life after death.

I read the book after Chris had died, and realised why she was so fascinated with it, and knew the intensity of her faith in the resurrection and how it made all the difference to her living these last months. And the book spoke to me of the wonder of resurrection, as I sought to come to terms with her death. God had guided me to buy the book for her as an Easter present, with no knowledge that it contained anything about resurrection.

During this time Chris spoke to our neighbour Mary about life beyond death. Mary had confessed to being scared of death and Chris said to her, "When you arrive at the shore beyond death, I will be waiting to greet you, Mary". I didn't know of this till many months later. There were many thoughts that Chris shared with others, but not me. Perhaps she guessed I would pick them up afterwards.

The South African elections were part of the backdrop of these nine days. We heard of Bishop Desmond Tutu dancing and saying: "We are the Rainbow People of God". On a walk in the countryside, they were in my mind. As I watched the newly returned swallows, and was excited as I heard the cuckoo quite close, I was suddenly struck by the realisation that they had recently flown from Africa - nature's link across the continents. I thought, too, of Dulwich Grove's link with Big Ada in Ghana, and Ruth Clarke's recent visit. I thought of the wonder of new life and new hope this Spring, mirrored by the bluebells and blossom, and the baby starlings growing in the nest under the cottage eaves, and put in my diary, "The Holy Spirit - the Power of God". It was an inspiring time.

On the Saturday we felt the power of God's spirit too, in a different way. It was to be another last meeting, fleeting but significant, for it was Brian Johanson's induction at Robertson Street URC, Hastings. We had heard that Marion had had a fall, and possibly a stroke. She was confined to a wheelchair but would be at the Induction with her husband. I was worried about a parking place, but need not have been. A car drew out, just as I got there, so I was able to help Chris inside up the steps, and Marion and Brian were just going in. Marion spotted Chris and waved and smiled, two people facing cancer cheerfully and with faith in God. No words were spoken, but there was a deep understanding between them. At the induction there were also prayers for healing - it was very moving. Brian and Marion had very caring, sensitive, loving people around them at this difficult time. Chris felt weak and wobbly and didn't feel up to staying to talk afterwards, but there had been a meeting; that was enough.

After the car had had its MOT (they found the reason for the scraping, grinding noise that had dogged us over our pilgrimage - a faulty wheelbearing) we had some outings. One was to the church at Battle for a concert including Elgar's *Sea Pictures*. It reminded us of listening to the world service for Tim's birthday message to his mum from Singapore, when he asked them to play *'The Land Where Corals Lie'*. Jennifer Miller sang the songs beautifully and it was a special time for us.

Another outing was to Rudyard Kipling's house, Batemans. Just before going, Chris and I got across one another. I think it was because I was getting anxious about getting back to work and how I would cope, especially with the Bromley District Presidency. I was writing my Pentecost sermons and getting worried about them, but I was also very worried about Chris's mobility. She couldn't seem to walk for more than 50 yards or so, and was very unsteady, but wouldn't take a higher steroid dose. So she got out to show me what she could do and walked all round the garden at Batemans, including right down to the mill. When she'd done that, I felt more at ease. I suppose I was really panicking because it was obvious the symptoms were returning in spite of the steroids, and that there was a limit to what the steroids could do to keep Chris going. Her death was drawing nearer, but her smile and determination did not waver. We had a lovely time at Batemans, the journey home was along a lane full of wild flowers, and we heard the cuckoo! Chris was so thrilled.

We went to Canterbury cathedral again - for Ascension Day. We went to the Christkindl Market and bought a little clock for Chris's birthday. We only just got there before it closed - they were just locking up, but unlocked again for us, and a little pendulum clock, hand-carved and painted, a bit like a tiny cuckoo clock without the cuckoo was purchased - just what Chris wanted. We had missed the service in the Cathedral but Chris sat down for a long time, and lit a candle for Sue who was expecting the baby any time. I found, in the church treasury, a kind of tapestry of gold and silver thread from Nicaea, depicting the burial of Jesus and used for the Good Friday vespers and Easter Midnight, and traditionally displayed till Ascension Day. We both looked at it and found it special for the day.

During this time Chris finished the matinee coat for the baby - a few more holes than there should be, perhaps, but it made it look lovely and lacey! She wanted to go and see *'Schindler's List'*. I said I couldn't cope with it - so instead we bought some garden chairs with the money and she made some cushions for them out of an old bit of bedding from the cottage; tartan, very suitable after our Scottish trip. And Chris bought me the book of *'Schindler's List'*. Having read some of it I was very glad I hadn't gone to see the film - not at this time.

And, of course, we heard of John Smith's death. It was a great shock to us. Nothing ever stays the same. Even when things seem very stable and reliable, there are shock changes.

We had some beautiful sunny days, and sat out and gained as much strength as we could from our lovely secret garden.

Eventually on cup final day, we had to leave. Chris packed bag after bag. I had decided that the M25 would be at its quietest during the cup final, so that's when we did our journey. We were off to Uxbridge so that we could be there on the Sunday when Dave and Ruth were being made members. It poured the whole of the journey, and it wasn't pleasant driving in the heavy rain and spray, but we got there, and after tea there was an evening of showing photos and slides.

So on the Sunday we met Robert and Joyce again who had come down from Coventry for the membership ceremony. Waterloo Road church has always been a 'mission', with no attachments to any denomination, but perhaps rather Baptist in style of worship. Afterwards we met up with Sue, Simon and Matthew - there'd been false alarms, but still no baby! Then we packed up for the last time, and went home to Dulwich.

It was a relief to get back after our three months away, and spend time trying to sort all the bags out. There was still a lot left at the cottage for future visits, but it was the end of any long stay there together. There was a lot of work waiting for me to do church-wise - a lovely 'Welcome Back' card from the church with lots of names on it, but before I started the church work I had a journey to do on my own. Chris was in no fit state to come with me and was still very unsteady. The trip was to Mill Hill to see my father, and on the way I called at Tumi's at Camden Town to pick up three scarves made in central America. It was Chris's idea to get them, to present to Dianna and Rosemary (local clergy) and Tim for their forthcoming ordinations. She had already given some money to Judith, who had bought a skirt to wear on the day. These ordinations were very important to Chris. Perhaps she felt that as she was giving up her ministry, so they were carrying on - the power of the Holy Spirit passing from Chris to them in a way. I don't know, but something made these ordinations very special for her, though of course Tim's was anyway for family reasons.

It was hard to explain to my father that Chris couldn't come. I think he found it very difficult to understand that his daughter-in-law was so handicapped now - it has always been him who couldn't do things. I'm sure he was very upset about it, as he thought a lot of Chris.

When I got back, Chris had coped, but was very glad to see me. Then the 'phone rang. It was Simon - but still no baby. Sue's waters had broken the night before, and she was in hospital, but nothing further had happened. It was a worrying time.

The next day there was still no news. Chris was feeling cold - we had the central heating on and a gas fire. She took a long time to get up, so I changed an appointment with George, my church secretary, from 10 am to 11 am to let her get up properly. I went with a very fat file, feeling pressurised by so much work to catch up on. I felt panicky about getting on top of it again. Then there was a surprise 'phone call - no, not the baby, but an old friend from two churches back, the scout leader there. He was in London, could he call and see us? It was great to see him - just like old times. He talked and talked as he always did. It was a lovely afternoon, and it took our minds off Sue.

Then there was the tea to prepare and the Elders Meeting to get ready for. It was a scramble and Chris found it difficult to help. After a really good elders meeting with people so helpful and glad to see me, I came home to find Chris wreathed in smiles: Simon had just 'phoned - it's a girl, Avril Helen, 9lb 4oz, by Caesarean. Sue was thrilled - one of each. Chris was so relieved - another goal - Grandma again. She seemed quite transformed.

The following day, after an interview about the baptism scheduled for Sunday morning at Dulwich Grove, we were off to Uxbridge to see our new grandchild. Sue and Chris had lots of tears and hugs. Matthew was there sharing in it all, Grandpa and Dad were very proud, and the camera recorded it all. What a lovely way to finish our pilgrimage.

Work was beginning to take a more normal course. I went off to the Thursday early morning prayers (at St John's). There was a reading from *2 Corinthians: 3* about the veil over Moses' face to cover God's glory shining there. That afternoon Chris was determined to do her hospital chaplaincy work. She took two bags, containing her communion set and her books, to give Olive communion. Olive had broken her hip on Valentine's Day, the day before our send-off, and was still in hospital after 3 months, all the time of our sabbatical. I dropped Chris off at the hospital and she staggered inside. I went off to do my chaplaincy work at Dulwich as I normally did, but I was worried about Chris, and went back for her early. She had managed - it was the last communion she did - indeed, the last service of any kind. Thank goodness one of my church members was there visiting Olive and could help. She was able to come with Chris to the hospital entrance to wait for the car. Chris was just totally determined to do her chaplaincy work, she refused to be beaten. The new grandchild had given her a lift - she was not going to give up living yet!

I was determined to help her cope and the next day I fixed a grab handle on the stairs so that she could pull herself up. I bought a telephone answering machine to save her trying to cope with 'phone calls while I was out. Both proved very valuable aids to help her live relatively normally. I was out in the evening at the Christian Aid Auction at church, which raised £3,470, and when I got back Chris had been baking, some little buns for Pentecost for the children to hold with a candle in for the Pentecost flames, and for them to eat afterwards, of course!

So it was eve of Pentecost Day - the day of the ordinations. I took the scarves round for Dianna and Rosemary, and a photocopy of information about them from Horniman's museum, where Chris had got the idea originally. They were very pleased with the thought. Dianna was on crutches, spondylitis, but was hoping she'd cope that night. I was very worried about parking at Southwark cathedral. I feared there'd be a long way to walk, but as at other times our prayers were answered. We actually got lost and I came to the cathedral by a back way, and there was a parking place, only 20 yards from the entrance - that **must** have been divine planning. The cathedral was almost full, how was that parking place still free?

The bells were ringing, and inside the cathedral looked beautiful - Chris thought it was a bit like Iona. We found some good seats where we could see well. Many people came up to talk to us, we felt very much at home with all our Anglican friends. There had been two previous ordination services that day, there were so many women to be ordained. One of those ordained I was to get to know better, one of the Chaplains at St Christopher's Hospice. The gospel reading was *John 20: 11-23*, about the resurrection and the giving of the Holy Spirit - so suitable for our pilgrimage. For me the high spot was when each candidate in turn moved to the centre of the tower space, accompanied by the priests who were to lay hands on her, along with the bishops. The bishop said, "Send down the Holy Spirit upon your servant (name) for the office and work of a priest in your church". Dianna (who had thrown away her crutches), Judith, Rosemary were the names we listened for. At the end everyone clapped, and there was a long sharing of the peace. It was wonderful. Chris was worried about getting to the place to receive the bread and wine, but she was fine on my arm. At the end we slipped out - we were near the door. Chris had got to another of her goals.

So Pentecost Sunday dawned, and we went off to Dulwich Grove with lots of bits and pieces to be used at the service. Chris had on her 'gown of glory' at last! It had arrived through the post, and lo and behold it was not primrose colour but Pentecost red! We took our shells that we had faithfully taken with us everywhere and I presented the church with my Pentecost poster from Turvey Abbey. The cakes with the candles were used to great effect. The choir sang two special items for Pentecost. I talked in the sermon about our helplessness and total dependence on God's power, basing it on 'Blessed are the poor in Spirit' - one of the Beatitudes read at Iona Abbey - and related it to times in our pilgrimage where it seemed as if our difficulties were too great to deal with, and then suddenly everything came right for us.

I thanked them for their prayers at 12 o'clock each day. I talked of the wonders of the natural world we had seen, of God's spirit working in producing the snow, rainbow, spring flowers, and the mountains. It was lovely to be back to talk to them again, and as part of the service two elders, Pat and Manda, were ordained, reminding me of the ordinations in the cathedral the night before. So we gathered around the Lord's Table, as we had done three months before on our send-off, and shared with each other the food of eternal life. Chris and I thanked God for our wonderful pilgrimage completed. At the end of the service Chris was surrounded by people, and she was showing them photos of Avril.

After a long afternoon, and the evening service (Chris stayed at home) we went down to the cottage, very tired, bearing flowers from the church. And Chris fell down on the steps. It was only a slight fall - her legs were getting weaker - or was it just tiredness? We got thankfully to bed in our lovely restful place of retreat. It had been quite a week.

PART IV
THE LAST TWO MONTHS

From Chris's Birthday to my Induction as President
May 23rd - June 7th 1994

It was good Chris's birthday was on a Monday that year - my day off. We determined earlier that, as far as possible, we would go down to our cottage on a Sunday night and return Tuesday morning, to have a proper day off. Chris stayed in bed on her birthday morning for a while and I got up and got into the garden. When I stopped for a rest she was up, so I came in to share the card and present opening. I had been careful buying my card: 'Many happy returns' was not appropriate, nor were some other usual birthday sentiments. She was pleased with what I did get. She got lots of other cards, and some 'Congratulations, Grandma' cards too! We fixed up the clock - not the best of timekeepers, but very pretty. She has always loved a clock with a loud tick. We spent some of the money she received on a celebration meal at the 'White Hart' up the road. She had an enormous mixed grill and ate the lot! I discovered we could successfully access the answerphone at Dulwich from the cottage, and there were a number of birthday wishes on it! The family rang the cottage too. She was very pleased with her day, but the next day at the District Executive committee I felt awful. I just didn't feel in touch with district things, and I couldn't see myself chairing one of these committees, let alone a big District Council meeting. I came back and told Chris how I felt. As usual she was understanding and encouraging- perhaps that almost made it worse, as I knew she wouldn't always be there to support me.

We had a visit from David Helyar the next day. He was lovely, talking to us and saying prayers for us about this difficult time. He was very reassuring too about support for me from the district and province. Then in the evening when I came back from a meeting I found the door chained and Chris in bed - I had a job to get her to come downstairs to unlock it. "I wondered where you were", she said, but her mind hadn't wondered enough to leave the door unchained. The next day we had 7.30 am clergy prayers at our house. Chris decided to get up for them, but then wasn't ready and I had to help her dress. During the prayers she suddenly lurched sideways and nearly fell out of the chair. Then at the breakfast she said, "Sorry I didn't make prayers". Her speech was a bit slurred. I got very worried and called the doctor. She came, the first time we had seen her since the Monday after that horrible day, when she was so straight with us, but helpful and gentle too. This time, too, she was very supportive and helpful. She said she would organise a nurse to come and visit and she doubled the steroid dose. Suddenly we were back with the medical people again. The freedom had only just lasted over the sabbatical period, a few days beyond it, and we were into visits and appointments. The timing had been exactly right yet it had been arranged over a year before. That was surely not coincidence. So the nurse came and began to talk about possibilities - maybe the bed would have to come downstairs. She brought a blue report book with her and filled part of it up. While she was here Judith came and after the nurse had gone we looked at the blue book! It was to be one of many visits and interviews with Judith over these next months. Chris was worried she couldn't get back to doing her chaplaincy work, and Judith reassured her that sick people were not expected to work. We asked her if she would do a house communion for us again, now she was ordained, and she agreed.

Everyone seemed to be coming to help. The vicar at the joint URC/C of E Copleston Centre, and his wife brought me a clematis called 'Mr President'! Helen arrived with birthday presents - books *'Cry Freedom'* and *'Mother Teresa'*. I read the latter during the next few weeks and found it really inspiring. It provided a few sermons.

On the Sunday there was a baptism - I always enjoy them, carrying the baby round the congregation! Chris came as usual. In spite of all the medics around we just carried on living and refused to let the illness get in the way, so off we went to the cottage in the evening as we tried to do each week.

It was Bank Holiday Monday. As a result of my having new tyres fitted on the car for the journey to Scotland, the Hastings garage had got my address, and sent me a special offer - have a test drive and get a £15 voucher. I'd fixed to do the test drive this bank holiday, thinking it would be a laugh, and £15 into the bargain. So off I went to do it. Of course they had the laugh on me because I ordered a new car! As it turns out, I've never regretted it, and it became very special because Chris agreed to give it to me as her leaving present. It came out of her money left to her by her parents years before. The whole transaction took a long time, with me going back to the cottage to think about it. Maybe it was another thing God had arranged for us, to get us through this period. It certainly took my mind off other things, though at the time Chris had hoped we'd have a day out at Batemans again. Maybe she was better having a rest and writing letters, but in her diary she put: "Had a bit of an anticlimax day! Couldn't manage Batemans."

At least we had a lovely sit in our new chairs in the garden in beautiful sunshine the next day, using the cushions she had made. Now our diaries began to have appointments to keep with nurses and doctors, so we had to go back home and see Nurse Lesley. She was trying to assess needs, mine as well as Chris's. She told Chris to apply for the Disablement Living Allowance. Chris filled in the form in her own unique style (she could never fill in forms without all kinds of comments) and then I found she'd filled in parts she shouldn't have! There was a contribution that the Doctor had to make, too, but she filled it in and sent it without letting me see what she had put. Needless to say, Chris was very curious to know why but even she didn't dare ask her.

The day after we were at King's College Hospital. We had to wait so long we thought they must have forgotten about us. It was a visit that had been fixed just after Easter, and it turned out to be a sad visit. The registrar saw us and she found it a hard interview, as we all did. There were the usual tests and examinations, and then she said, "Do you really want to keep coming here? There's nothing more we can do really. Would you be better seeing the nurses and your GP?" And we agreed - very sadly. It was another last time. We put on our badges as chaplains and went off to the canteen for lunch and saw lots of people we knew. It was a support place for us as well as an outpatient's consultation. As we were coming away we met some friends - their baby was on its way and they were going up to the labour ward. We wished them the very best.

That evening I spoke to the Cloister (sheltered housing) about our pilgrimage together. I took a whole lot of stones and told the story through these. It went really very well and, of course, they were all asking about Chris.

The next day the doctor came. Chris and I were amazed at all the medical attention we were getting. Chris said to me, "Do they know something we don't know?" It was suggested that as Chris was finding it difficult to get up the stairs now, and seemed to need some sleep during the day, it might be a time to bring the bed downstairs. In any case, it would be necessary later on. Chris was asked if she wanted to be at home or in the hospice for her last days, and she opted to be at home.

It was decided that Chris's study was the best place for the bed. It would just fit and she would not be 'on view' to the neighbourhood as she would in the front room. It was handy for the loo, and the kitchen would just have to make do for any washing facilities. It was not ideal, but certainly possible.

The next day Chris began to sort out her study. It must have been very painful for her. It was always her special place and I had never intruded there. She had her 'phone, her table for working, her books, her messy papers all over the floor, her cards and pictures displayed, and now I was in there measuring up, and saying what would go where. She threw a lot of things away and made piles of fat files, and put things in drawers, but as far as possible it remained a study, and she asked me to put up her little clock from Canterbury. Then the 'phone rang: our friends we'd met at the hospital had had a little girl, Hannah. Chris became chaplain again, "Let's go and see her, and maybe they would like some prayers". So off we went, and as usual I was wondering how I was going to park near enough for her to manage. I needn't have worried. There was a spot just outside the main entrance. I have never before or since got a place there - it is always full of cars, but there it was, waiting for us - and I knew it was not coincidence. Chris managed to get to the ward, though it's a fair distance in the hospital, and of course she met people. We bought an African violet plant for them, and admired, and said prayers. Chris was so pleased to go - she was still able to live normally and share in people's celebrations.

Then it was Saturday and I went off to the church Coffee Morning with instructions to buy cakes for the family coming on Monday. While I was there Barry came to visit Chris. He was an elder at Camberwell Green church, and had arranged to come. They talked and prayed together about the church, and the special church meeting the next day about its future. It was good that I was out for Camberwell Green church was Chris's special place, and I did not want to interfere. Barry brought her a book called *'The Celtic Vision'* about Hebridean prayers and blessings. It was from this book that Chris copied out a few quotations and put them together for Barry to read at her funeral. It must have been soon after this time that she did it. She was now finding books very heavy to hold. It was only a week after this that she wrote the last entry in her diary, and I have not found anything else she wrote later than this.

To me it is quite miraculous that Chris found the quotes all on a double page spread of the book. For I recognise references to many stages of our pilgrimage together, to holidays in Wales, and our honeymoon in Ireland, as well as her death and resurrection, not specifically, of course, but by inference in different ways. It is all definitely there and Barry brought that book only just in time for her to do it. At the funeral it made a very great impression, Simon's father being almost too overcome to play Simon's accompaniment straight afterwards, and everyone thought Chris had written it herself, it was so apt (it is quoted later in this book).

It was about this time that Chris said to me, "John, can we go over the funeral together now, please", and of course I did. It was very hard to do, and yet very wonderful too. I had no idea what she had put in that drawer. It was pretty roughly done, with bits and pieces added together, but the ideas were all there, and we talked about who would do what - or rather, she told me! She knew exactly what she wanted. Even then I couldn't bring myself to look up the bible readings. I just satisfied myself I knew everything she wanted, and she was satisfied I understood and would arrange it as she had planned it.

There was a feeling again of drifting apart, as there was back in February. She was still on her spiritual journey, sorting herself out for death. I was necessarily dealing with the practicalities - bed-moving, study sorting, and the details of the funeral service. She was seeing the spiritual visions of her death and funeral. I was the stage manager; she was writing and acting out the drama. I am convinced that as she sorted her study papers, there were some she deliberately left for me to find later, so that I could write this. It was a part of her vision that it should be written up later, though we never spoke about it.

On the Sunday she came to Dulwich Grove. Helen was home and helped her in. She enjoyed talking to everyone but her mind, I'm sure, was on the Camberwell Green church meeting. Would they decide to close? She got the news - no, they were going to go on, looking to the neighbouring churches for help. Chris was so relieved - it meant such a lot to her.

On the Monday, Sue, Simon, Matthew and Avril arrived, and Simon and I were able to bring the bed downstairs. We took her study table out, and replaced it with a smaller table with a top that wiped down and wouldn't spoil with bowls of water, soap, and medical equipment, covering it with the Indian cloth that had been on the other table and it looked fine. Sue decided to bring Avril's baptism forward to June 26th so that her Mum could be there. It was a difficult decision because the Godparents, Tim and Helen were not able to be there. But she felt she was right, and never regretted it. It gave Chris another goal to aim at, and she started knitting a little hat for Avril. It never ever really looked like a hat, and she never finished it, but she stuck at it, determined she would not be beaten, however much people might laugh at her strange creation! That evening we went to a service at the Maudsley Hospital chapel, by special request. Rosemary, recently ordained at the Cathedral, and chaplain to the hospital, was officiating at her first communion as priest. It was a lovely gathering. Dianna and Judith were there, ordained with Rosemary, along with many others, including Charlotte who had lent Chris the book *'Getting Well Again'*, and Cecil who had brought me *'Mr President'*. The chapel is very small, but was full to overflowing, and it was a very special time for all of us.

And so the day dawned for me to be inducted as president of the Bromley District Council of the URC. The date had been known for such a long time. It was 18 months before that I had been asked, just a week or so before Chris had found the lump in her breast. It was the reason for the timing of the sabbatical - which had been so crucial. Even a week either way would not have been so good - it had been perfectly timed - divine timing. Janice came in the morning, a new nurse, replacing Lesley due to reorganisation with Lesley introducing her to us.

I was very uptight about the induction which was to be at Dulwich Grove. I was very worried about my ability to chair such a large meeting afterwards. I think a lot of people were very sympathetic because of the circumstances. Chris came to the service, but went home after the refreshments and before the business meeting. My church treasurer was to take her home and see she was all right. She was a bit upset as some of her friends did not recognise her. She had changed a lot, the steroids were really affecting her badly. All went well and the service was fine. The meeting seemed to go quite well, though I was glad when it was over. It was another of Chris's goals, her last District Council, and the last time she would meet a lot of her friends, and she had chatted to a lot of people from the District she knew so well.

The next day was my Dad's birthday. He had hoped we might get over to see him but he didn't realise how impossible it was. Judith came and officiated at a house communion as she had the day we left on our pilgrimage. This time she was ordained and used the words of consecration.

Two days later we were at Dulwich Grove again, this time for our first report from the Pilgrimage to the church. Chris came, and joined in with my talk. I showed half of the slides, and talked about the pilgrimage and the natural world: the views, mountains, and secret garden etc., leaving the spiritual side to the next evening, fixed for three weeks later. The hall was full of people - it was a lovely occasion of sharing.

I have written this chapter as a diary, because it shows the intensity of our living. It was an amazing time with everything happening in very quick succession. It was so important that it all happened like this, because Chris was still well enough to be involved. We were still living on a 'higher plane' than normal, and all the special occasions kept us both going. But Chris was continuing to get weaker. Her ankles swelled, she found it difficult to do things, and I helped her more and more, like putting her tights and shoes on for her. She was having to rest more, using the bed downstairs, and I had to arrange handholds so that she could pull herself out of it.

She talked about the hymn book at church being too heavy to hold and for a long time now she had not stood up for the hymns. Fortunately she was able to get in and out of the car, with a certain amount of help, but often she would call from the loo for me to pull her up on to her feet. Sometimes she could manage, sometimes not. At the cottage she was using the back door to get in and out now, where the steps were easier, and I fixed handholds there for her.

But through this period, she remained cheerful, with a radiant smile for everyone and never was sorry for herself. Sometimes she would get annoyed at her weakness, and shout 'pig, pig' as the tights or shoes wouldn't go on for her, but she didn't complain and always her concern was for other people. People had always been her main interest, and always she was curious as to what they were doing, interested almost to a fault in other people's affairs. It stood her in good stead now.

The Period Before the Hospice

I have a letter Chris wrote to friends in Harrow, written on the Saturday. From it, you would not guess she was so very ill but she is obviously aware her brain is playing her tricks:

"Dear Noel and Ann

Thanks for your message. Sorry about the Ansaphone - but it's one of the ways we are coping! (when we remember to switch it on!).
Congrats on the new arrival (to Claire) and of course Naomi to Laurent and your daughter.
My brain is not too bad - but I get very forgetful and mixed up (sometimes I forget I've been to a meeting or prayers! Once I locked John out, not realising it was an evening meeting! and today at 3.0 pm I thought it was 3.0 am!)
But our journeys North challenged and stimulated me greatly!
We have been discharged from K C H into the hands of St Christopher's team (and the GP). Both are very helpful, lovely girls, I call them! (like the radiotherapy girls).
Simon has helped John to bring my bed downstairs for afternoon rests!
Sue had a baby girl on May 17th (Avril Helen) 9lb 4oz - born by Caesarean of course! All went well, (both are well) and she is very placid.
Matthew loves her and is quite a tornado! They all came on Monday - which was wonderful, but exhausting! (Especially as we had an early evening meeting).
Tomorrow Dave and Ruth are coming over to cook Sunday lunch for us (and to come to Dulwich Grove with us too!). The family are rallying round wonderfully!
The baptism for Avril will be June 26 all being well (at Christchurch, Uxbridge).
How is your mother? Well, we hope!
So thanks again for your love and support!
Christine and John xx"

On the Sunday she watched Roy Castle's *'Sweet Inspiration'* on the television. She thought a great deal of him, and drew inspiration from him in her attitude to her illness. Then we were off to the cottage, and the next day she got her visit to Batemans after all. We picked up the new car in Hastings, and took it on its first run there. It was a struggle, but she managed to get to the restaurant and the shop, but not the mill this time. It was very difficult back up the hill to the car park. She was very pleased with the car, and the garage had given her a gorgeous bunch of flowers too. That night I left her at the cottage, with David and Mary, from next door keeping an eye on her so that the next day I could bring my church secretary, George, and one of my church members, Yvonne, down to look at the Adelphi Hotel, Hastings, where our church weekend away was to take place in October. Arrangements were being finalised, and it was important for them to see the hotel. Chris was fine, and we called in to the cottage for coffee. Neither of them had seen the cottage before. Chris's idea was that on the Sunday afternoon of the weekend away all the folk would visit the cottage on the way back to Dulwich. We had lunch together at Battle after the hotel visit, and then went back home. It was a lovely day together, and I had also given the car a good try-out before leaving Hastings.

During this week we had another important lunch, with the clergy of the churches concerned with helping at Camberwell Green. It was held at the manse so that Chris could be there. She was glad still to be involved. We had various other visits, one being a home visitor from St Christopher's Hospice. There was very good communication between the GP, the nurses, and St Christopher's, and about this stage the visitor came with a message from King's College Hospital. Would Chris like to consider having a further head scan, to see if drainage could be arranged to relieve the brain of the pressure caused by the tumour? It would not be a cure, but might have a palliative effect. When Chris was asked, the 'phone rang and I went to answer it.

When I got back, she had given her answer: no, she wanted no further scans or hospital treatment. She was still facing her death calmly and serenely. She was not afraid. She was in control.

Geoffrey and Betty, my brother and his wife, came. We had a lovely chat, looking at the photo album. Chris was very much on form - it was a really good visit.

That Saturday Chris surprised everyone by going to the 'Cause for Celebration' and staying the whole day. It was a excellent annual multi-racial inter-church event held this time at Brockley. She went with two other ladies from Dulwich Grove while I was taking a wedding. The wedding went on a long time, everything was late, and I was amazed to find she wasn't back when I got home. She'd had a lovely time, and everyone there was inspired by her determination, and her interest in everything and everybody.

The following Monday Tim came down to the cottage from Grimsby to pick up my old car. I had offered it to him at the price the garage were prepared to give me in part exchange. He had finished his final exams at college and he was able to have a long chat with us that afternoon and evening and the following morning. It was a precious time for us all. Tim was so far away that face to face visits were not often possible. Again, Chris was on form. The next time Tim was to see his Mum was at the hospice, when she was not very with it at all.

That week we had a visit from a person from occupational health, who tried to assess alterations at the house to help Chris's mobility. She brought some high loo seats, which helped considerably for a little while. Chris was thrilled she didn't have to ask for help any more. Other aids that were planned came just too late. It takes time to organise the fitting of rails, and Chris's weakness got worse quite rapidly.

At the elders meeting at our house Chris was in her bed in the study, and the elders went in to talk to her after the meeting.

She had stopped writing now for every time she got out pen and paper to write letters she fell asleep. It was difficult for her to get out of bed on her own, and increasingly she was sleeping, so I had to be on hand to get her up when she woke.

But there were still special times to come. One of these was Avril Helen's baptism. On the Saturday I had a service at St Paul's Cray at 4 pm, so we were not able to leave for Uxbridge until the evening. I felt it was better to stay overnight than to try to do the double journey in a day, but I was very anxious that night, waiting for Chris to wake in the dark and try to get out of bed for the bathroom. I was worried she would fall in a strange place. All was well - I heard her getting up and was able to help.

In the morning she was still trying to finish the baby's bonnet. What she was creating was very strange, with bits of cloth sewn on and eventually she was persuaded to let Sue finish it. Sue has kept it as she left it, a witness to how Chris's brain was working, and how determined she was. The baptism was lovely, Chris took a photo and afterwards she talked a lot. Sue's friends were amazed at her, they could not believe she was so ill - they said: "She remembered things about us we had forgotten". It was a wonderful occasion - she was radiant, full of smiles, entering into the candle lighting and cake cutting. She held Avril and looked so proud to be a Grandma again.

She was buoyed up by the occasion, and when we had got back to Dulwich and I was taking the evening service, she was sorting out things to get to the cottage that evening. She helped get the meal ready when we got there, and I think I was fooled into thinking she was better since she was managing so well. She was late getting up, so I went in the garden to cut a hedge for a while, and spoke to the neighbours. When I went in to see how she was doing, I heard her shout from the bathroom. She had fallen into the bath. She said she'd been there half an hour and had hit her head. There was no sign of any injury and fortunately the taps weren't on. I felt dreadfully guilty for leaving her. I had a difficult job getting her out but eventually managed it without doing either of us an injury.

But we both knew it was the last time we'd be at the cottage together. I have little recollection of how we got home, or how I cleared up the cottage for a long time away from it. The fall had either sapped Chris's confidence, or perhaps it was a sudden deterioration that had caused the fall, but suddenly I had everything to do.

All that week she slept, in between meals or getting to the bathroom. She could not get up the stairs, so at night I had to listen hard to hear if she was trying to get up, which she couldn't do by herself. Every meal she managed to get to the table - though on one occasion she said to me, "It feels really funny having breakfast here!" - the same place as she'd had it every day for 6 years! I was not able to go out unless someone was there with her. Church work became very difficult, although people were helping a lot. On the Friday there was our presentation of Pilgrimage Part 2, *'The Spiritual Journey'*, and she was determined to come. In the hall she struggled to a chair with a lot of help, and took part in it all - never once did she close her eyes. The Ghanaian choir, who had wanted to come to the house that evening, came to the meeting instead and sang while we had the refreshments. At the end, as they sang their recessional song, each of them went up to Chris and gave her a kiss. The hall was packed with folk entering into the wonderful spiritual experience we'd had. And the radiant smile was there again! She was centre stage, and her happiness helped everyone to be happy. People saw the light of heaven in her eyes, not the weakness of her body.

That week the *'Commitment for Life'* banner was delivered to our house, now completely finished, with beautiful embroidery. Chris was thrilled to see it finished at last. It seemed such a long time since she'd bought the kit. Then Judith came with a framed picture of Chris in the hospital chapel in her finery, with the other chaplains and Bishop Simon Phipps at the rededication some months before. Stuart had had it framed by some people on the hospital staff. It was a tribute to her work over the years. Helen and Andy came for the weekend, and Sue, Simon and the children arrived on the Sunday and we all went to church. I had a terrible job getting Chris out of my car when we got there. She'd had a headache that morning, the first one for months. Maybe it was the painkillers she'd taken for the headache but she was nearly a dead weight to pull out of the car. But she got there, and saw the new banner installed in the church, and thanked the ladies for doing it. We had a lovely meal together, and a good afternoon chatting away as if nothing was wrong!

But now came a problem. Chris had arranged that while I was at the URC Assembly in Lancaster she would stay in Coventry with Robert and Joyce. It had been arranged a long time and it was very convenient. I would drop her off on the way up, and pick her up on the way back, but the medics said "No". I said, "Well, I'd better not go to the Assembly". But Chris, still in charge, said "Of course you're going. As President of the District you must". There was no arguing with Chris, she was quite adamant.

So it was St Christopher's Hospice to the rescue! Somehow they found a bed for her, and she went in on the Wednesday, the day before I was due to drive up to Lancaster. It was for a week's respite care.

St Christopher's Hospice

I went up with Chris in the ambulance. They took her in a chair and she was in a bay with three others. When I went to see her in the evening, one of the staff asked me, "Was she walking when she came in?" I explained she'd come in a chair. "No, I mean, could she walk?" "Well, yes, she was able to get to the loo, once I'd got her off the bed". "Well, it took two nurses, one each side, this afternoon. Her legs were buckling under her". She'd got there just in time, but I didn't realise that then.

That night I got back to an empty house. It didn't hit me too hard as I was off to the Assembly at 6 o'clock the next morning with George, my church secretary. We had a good drive up, and I met many friends. Everyone was so concerned, and amazed that I'd come. I was glad David Helyar, my moderator, had come to see us in Dulwich and could confirm that I'd had my orders from Chris and had to come.

Away from the business meeting my time was spent in talking to so many people. I made a list, because I knew when I rang Chris she'd be asking - who did you see?, what did they say?, how is so-and so? I rang three times a day and each time I said, "Are you all right? Do you want me to come back?", and each time she said, "Of course you must stay".

Suddenly she changed - on the evening of the second day. I rang her, and she said, "Are you coming in tonight?" I had to explain where I was. "Do you want me to come back?" "Yes please, I do miss you". Nothing could stop me. I told one or two I was going, fixed up a lift for George to get back, and set off. In fact, I'd been to a lot of what I was interested in anyway, and seen so many people, it had been well worth going. I got back after midnight. Tim and Rebekah had come down to see her too.

Chris was very confused the next day, but the smile of welcome and the "Oh, John, it's lovely to see you" was worth the long drive through the night.

On the Sunday I took a little radio in and we listened together to the broadcast service from the Assembly.

Her confusion may well have been due to her blood sugar level going out of control - another effect of the steroids. But I felt it right to let Helen know what was happening, she had left her telephone number where she was on holiday. She came with Andy on the Tuesday, and it was on that day I had an interview with the hospice doctor. He told me that it would be quite impossible to get her home again, she was too weak to travel, and it wouldn't be possible to fix up the care she needed at home. She was now on a special bed.

That Wednesday I paced up and down the house. Chris had wanted to be at home. I was going to let her down. What could I do? What would I say when she asked me? I went over and over it in my brain - we'd never had secrets from each other but she was pretty confused and perhaps she wouldn't know, maybe she wouldn't ask. That night I went in to see her, and she smiled at me and said, "John, I know I can't come back tonight, but it will be lovely to see my little study again tomorrow with my little clock". Just at that moment Judith came in. I lost count of how many times she came, or rang up to find out how things were going. I said to Chris, "You talk to Judith, I'll see the staff nurse". So I went to the office and asked, "Is there any chance of Chris coming home?" "No, I'm afraid not - it just isn't possible". "All right, I'll go and tell her - she's asking". "Do you want me to come with you?" "No, thanks, we've always been able to be honest with each other".

So when Judith went, I said, "Chris, you know you were asking about coming home? Well, they say it isn't possible. You're too weak". She looked at me - but instead of tears there was a smile. We held each other, and I said, "It's the last stage of the pilgrimage". She said, "Yes. I hope it isn't too long". We both understood each other perfectly. The pilgrimage was nearing its close, and I couldn't be the stage manager any longer. It was in the hands of the hospice, and in the hands of God.

The next day I told Helen and Andy to put the bed back upstairs. I had to recognise she was not coming back home. They did it while I was out, and when I came back I looked in the study and felt very shocked. She was going away from me. Our pilgrimages were going in different directions. But the radiance was in her eyes. Everyone said it who went to see her - she is so serene, she is so calm, she asked after everyone, she's so concerned about everybody. One person said, "It was me that was sad, she's not sad at all".

I carried on with the church work. Chris would have been upset if I hadn't, just as she wanted me to go to the assembly. People asked me if they could visit. "Of course", I said. "But don't wake her if she's fast asleep". I went in morning, afternoon and late evening usually. Sometimes she didn't wake for me, and I didn't wake her. I don't know everyone who visited, but flowers and cards kept arriving - some she knew about and some she didn't, and everyone felt her peace and happiness, and the wonder of that beautiful place. She attended a communion there, though she didn't tell me - I found out later. I started going to the morning prayers there sometimes, led by different people each day.

At the weekend I was able to take a wedding at the church and enjoyed taking it. There was a very big service on the Sunday - seven Ghanaian young people were being confirmed and coming into membership, and the church was packed - even half the gallery was full. Always when I went in, I would tell her all that was happening.

One day she said to me, "John, can we go to the cottage today?" I said, "Chris, there's no way I can get you to the car to take you, but shut your eyes and imagine it - the curtains, the table, the rose over the archway, your bedroom with the view". She smiled and shut her eyes and said, "I'm good at imagining".

But one thing was wrong and we had to face it together. She had one last goal which she was not going to manage. I had to face her with it. "Chris", I said, "I'm afraid you're not going to get to Tim's ordination". She opened her eyes wide. "Why not?" she said sharply. "Well", I said, "You can't get out of bed. If you did I couldn't get you into the car. Even if I did that, you have no strength to survive the journey to Huddersfield. It's impossible. I'm sorry, but I'm afraid you can't be there". She looked at me with the eyes of one used to being in control of things. "Don't you be too sure", she said. And as people talked to me months later about their conversations with her, several said how worried they were about her certainty that she would be at the ordination. She was quite determined. She slept more and more, though some visitors found her suddenly awake, and perfectly lucid. On the Saturday Helen and I went to the hospice in the morning. There was no sign of any consciousness and we talked to each other. Then I fancied Chris's eyes moved slightly. I asked, "Are you listening to us?". There was just the faintest of nods - we both saw it. We talked to her, then, but there was no further movement. When I went again, later in the day, she was fast asleep. That night Helen, Andy and I played a game of cards, and we enjoyed it. That day the church had been to Brighton on the church family outing, and everyone had had had a good time, but when I went up to the hospice very late - she was restless but quite unconscious.

PART V
THE END OF THE PILGRIMAGE AND
MY JOURNEY BEYOND

Sunday, July 24th

I woke at 6 am to the sound of the telephone ringing. When it rings at that time it is something urgent and important. It was the hospice. I stood there in my study, out of breath and dazed after getting up in a hurry. There had been a change in Chris. They felt they should call me now, because they knew I would have commitments, it being a Sunday, and they wanted to give me time to arrange things. Helen and Andy joined me - they had heard the 'phone too. I told them the message. I was quite calm and I went down to have a quick breakfast. There on the table was the Morning Prayer. 'Lord, help me to remember that nothing is going to happen to me today that you and I together can't handle'. I got off to the hospice as quickly as possible, telling myself to drive carefully.

Chris's breathing was different. Her hand was very cold, even her face and head were cold. There was no response to me, talking or touching. She was very deeply unconscious. I sat there for a while, and talked to the staff. Chris had been restless overnight, so they had given her a sedative. It was strange sitting there - the other patients in the bay asleep or only half awake. It was a lovely sunny morning, and everything felt very special. There were the flowers and the plants and the cards Chris had received. It was very peaceful.

Then I realised it was Sunday, that I was due to take the service at 11 am, and that I was not going to be able to. My place was at the hospice. I had to go back home and arrange things. I talked to Matthew, one of the staff, and told him I would be back as soon as possible. He warned me that she might die while I was away, but it was a risk I had to take.

Quickly I drove back and made phone calls. I 'phoned David, our church treasurer, who is a lay preacher and could take the service if necessary. I left it to him to make arrangements, but suggested he get in touch with Lesslie who had offered to fill in for me at any time. I 'phoned Sue, who was due to come over anyway, and suggested that she might come earlier than planned.

Then I went back to the hospice. I felt I needed someone to say prayers with me, and looked round for one of the chaplains. I was told Len would be in soon - he had to come and do a service. They made me a cup of tea. I don't know how long I sat there. On such occasions time means nothing. I wandered about, looking at the beautiful pictures on the wall all around, with Jesus portrayed in dazzling white in all of them, and many of them suggesting the resurrected Jesus. I looked at the St Christopher's logo all over the place, with St Christopher holding the little child and taking him across the river. It is the whole purpose of the hospice - helping people on their journey across the river, and Chris would cross it today. Then I saw Len. He was just coming in. I asked him if he would say prayers with me, and he told me he'd come up soon.

The staff gave Chris a wash - it was all part of the routine. I'd been there before at this time and had to wait while it was done. At this time I 'phoned Tim and he asked me what she'd been like overnight. I told him she had been restless, throwing her arms about a bit. He said, "Yes, that's how she was as I was dreaming of her last night". When they had finished washing her her breathing was different again. Len came and said a prayer for us both, and afterwards asked if there was anything else he could do, anyone he could contact. On an impulse I asked him to try to contact Judith. She had not been in my mind till that moment.

I asked the staff how long they thought it would be before Chris died, but no-one knew - of course they didn't - it was a question I knew they couldn't answer. I just wanted reassurance, someone to talk to.

Then Judith arrived and it was good to see her. Almost immediately the telephone rang. It was for me - it was Dave. He was on holiday and out of reach by 'phone directly but somehow we'd got word through to him. I talked to him of the situation. He said he and Ruth would get back from Christchurch where they were as soon as they could. Then Matthew, the nurse, came in looking agitated. "Quickly", he said, "she's taking her last breaths". I told Dave I'd got to go, put the 'phone down and ran. I was just in time.

Judith stood by me, supporting me, and began:

"The Lord is your Shepherd, you shall not want. He makes you to lie down in green pastures; he leads you beside the still waters; He restores your soul. He leads you in the paths of righteousness for his name's sake. Yes, though you walk through the valley of the shadow of death, you will fear no evil. God is with you. His rod and staff will comfort you. He has prepared a table before you in the face of those that trouble you. He will anoint your head with oil and your cup will be full. Surely goodness and mercy will follow you all the days of your life. And you will dwell in the house of the Lord for ever".

I had never heard it said like that. Was she saying it for me or for Chris? - I suppose it was both of us, but individually, for we were on our separate journeys now. Judith went on praying, but I forget the words now. We were two ministers, looking down at a minister who was going through the miracle of death, just as wonderful and special as birth. I have often wondered why people are afraid of it. It is a moment when time and eternity meet, and where God is very close. I bent down and kissed what was no longer Chris. I looked up at Judith and thanked her and kissed her. I couldn't help myself. She was so special arriving in time to share these moments with me. I said, "That was good timing". She said, "It was divine timing". And we both knew it was true. God was working amongst us.

I looked up at the clock. It was 10.30. In half an hour the service at Dulwich Grove would start. I asked Judith if she could tell them what had happened, and she dashed off in her car.

I stood outside the curtain, and the lady in the opposite bed spoke to me. I told her Chris had died. She said, "Why does such a beautiful person have to die?" There is no answer to that question. I went back to sit by the bed, wondering what to do, and then Sue appeared. "She's gone", I said. We hugged one another and shed tears. It was the first of many emotional meetings. Afterwards she told me how Simon had dropped her off at the hospice door. They had the children with them, of course, so he couldn't come with her. She had found the journey up the stairs to the ward very difficult and she felt very alone. She also said afterwards she was glad her Mum had died before she got there, otherwise she would have been the only one of our children who had seen her die, and she didn't want that. Somehow what happened was right.

Simon took the children to the house and met Helen and Andy. They were about to go to church when I had rung and told them the news. Just then Judith arrived at the house and picked them up to take them up to the hospice. She'd already been to the church to tell them there.

Lesslie was taking the service, as only he could at a moment's notice. He had given us our shells of pilgrimage as we started out. Now he was sharing the end of the pilgrimage with the congregation. It was right that it was him.

George, in the notices, told the church of a special birthday too - Edna's mother in Jamaica was 110! And then she died the same day, too! How strange!

Matthew at the hospice was giving us tea and talking to us, and then we learnt that Judith was back with Helen and Andy. So we all met up, and Judith said some prayers for all the family. She didn't forget anyone, remembering everyone's name and who they were. I admired her incredible memory. And the prayers were just perfect. If I had planned the manner of Chris's death, it could not have been better. I was sure God had planned it.

Eventually we got home and had some lunch. The 'phone kept ringing, and we made some calls. I learned from Cecil at the Copleston Centre that they were praying for Chris at 10.30, just as she died. That was not coincidence, I'm sure, and he felt the same.

At 10.30 also, Tim and Rebekah were at a service in Huddersfield to admit them into membership of the church before Tim's ordination on Saturday. Chris, as minister, had just left this world, as Tim was about to become a minister. It was all connected together, weaving the picture, putting together the pieces of the jigsaw.

And then Dave and Ruth arrived, after a long drive. I went with them to the hospice, and we stayed a little while.

It was a sunny day, and we played with little Matthew in the garden, and nursed Avril! The younger generation couldn't be serious for long. We enjoyed each others company in the sunshine at this very special time. We all felt very emotional and shocked but also felt somehow at peace. Didn't Mary find the resurrected Jesus in the garden?

That evening it so happened that it had been arranged for Judith to do the evening service at Dulwich Grove. There was a larger than normal congregation, and she preached on the 23rd Psalm. 'It so happened'? No it was right - it had to be - God had planned it. As Judith had taken the house communion with us just before we left on our pilgrimage so she was intimately involved with the end of our pilgrimage. Another part of the picture.

It was a beautiful day in every way - the first day of the week - the day of resurrection. I felt I had glimpsed a little of heaven, as Chris left this world on her heavenly journey.

That evening the television programme *'Sweet Inspiration'* was based on the work of Dame Cicely Saunders at St Christopher's Hospice. There were pictures of the entrance and the wards, and the Triptych of pictures on the wall of the chapel, of Christ's birth, death, and resurrection. Dame Cicely was interviewed and spoke of her relationship with dying people, and the importance of the message they could convey as they died, and of her sharing in part with their feeling of going on beyond death on their journey. What she said spoke very much to me and my experience that day. When the family had gone home, Helen and Dave stayed with me. It was a warm evening and we went outside in the twilight, enjoying the garden and the quietness. We saw the owls flying about, and heard them hooting, and remembered how had Chris hated owls. In her upbringing she had learnt the superstition that they were a sign of death. Whenever she mentioned it, I used to point out that they had to live somewhere, and that they were lovely, fascinating creatures. Now she had faced death, accepted it, and gone through it in a wonderful way. Her way of death was not to be feared - it was beautiful. And we thanked God that her death was without pain or struggle. And if for us at that moment the owls were a symbol of her death, they were none the less lovely and fascinating for all that.

For many families, the death of a loved one can be very different - a sudden terrible accident, or days of suffering pain in spite of the painkillers, or a period when the person loses their mental capacity to make sense of their surroundings. Such experiences can be very tragic and hard to bear.

For our family this was not a tragedy, but a beautiful story with a beautiful end, pointing to the beauty of heaven beyond. For me, our pilgrimage together has been a gift from God, and in these pages I have tried to share the wonder of it.

The First Week, the Ordination and the Funeral

It was lovely to have Helen and Dave there for the first night. Somehow I managed to sleep and I stayed in bed till 'Thought for the Day' and the first part of the news, as we generally did. I knew it was important to keep a routine going. After breakfast we had a consultation. One of the most difficult questions was 'Which is to be first, the funeral or Tim's ordination?'. The more I had thought, overnight, the more I realised there would be no time to plan the funeral, and let everyone know, if it was held before the ordination. Though it would be hanging over us at the ordination, it couldn't be helped, the funeral had to come afterwards. I rang the undertakers, and David Helyar, whom Chris wished to lead the funeral, and it was fixed for Wednesday at 2 pm in nine days time. Then I had to go off to the hospice, pick up forms, and Chris's things, and have a chat and thank people, and then go to the Bromley office for registering the death, and then to the undertakers to sort out a lot of details. This part I didn't find difficult - it was very familiar ground to me, and I felt confident and decisive. There was also the family to ring to let them know the day and time, and the church so that things could be planned.

Helen and Dave asked me what they could do while I was away. I set Helen to a very difficult task, sorting out her mother's clothes, so that they could be bagged and taken to the hospice shop. She kept the special ones, and made up lots of grey bags of the rest. It was very hard for her, I'm sure. But later on, one night, she had a dream. She and her mother were in the bedroom investigating the wardrobe and Chris was saying to her, "Yes Helen, I think you've done a very good job with that". It is strange what happens to bereaved people. Helen found that dream very comforting. Dave, I set to work looking through Chris's plans for the funeral - to make up a service that would include it all, as far as possible in the order she had sketched it out, and I also asked him to draft out a letter to be duplicated and sent to our friends. He made a very good job of both these tasks. After tea when David Helyar arrived we looked at all the material Chris had left, and the order Dave had sorted out. I think David was a bit taken aback by the amount of material to go into the service, and wondered if it could all be contained in an hour. I wonder whether he had ever seen anything quite like it before for a funeral service, taped music, two organists, the Ghanaian choir, lots of people taking part, but we felt under orders. Chris had written this and it was all very clear what she wanted. There was really no argument.

It was on this day that I first saw some of the material, particularly what she had written for Barry from Camberwell Green to say. Where had she got it from? To me it sounded a bit disjointed, and at first I couldn't make real sense of it. Had she written it herself? It didn't seem her style.

'The Creator is seen in and through the world of His creating!
The goodness of God healed and restored the whole of Creation.
I arise today through strength of Heaven -
and there is a tree of apples of great bounty
a pretty bush - thick as a fist - of small hazel nuts.
The sound of the wind against a branching wood, grey cloud, river falls,
the cry of the Swan, delightful music!
The clear glass at the back of the church draws one's attention
from the communion table to the world outside! -
And I noticed the priest's eyes
As if he or she unknowingly put their hands on these gifts
As if these gifts of nature (and people) were the bread and the wine!
And so to the Cry of the Swan!'

Immediately afterwards Simon was to play *'The Swan'*, from *'The Carnival of the Animals'* by Saint-Saens, on his cello.

I looked long at it and couldn't reckon it up. What did it mean? It was four months before I found out where it came from, it was a remarkable welding together of Celtic poetry from Ireland, Wales and the Hebrides. It makes a piece that brings memories of Skye, and the cottage, together with Dulwich Grove and Coventry Cathedral, with their clear glass back windows, and the women and men priests sharing together at the communion table. There is her resurrection 'I arise today through strength of heaven', and there is the beautiful music made by the dying swan - surely herself.

It was one of the last things she wrote - pieces taken from one page spread of the introduction to *'The Celtic Vision'* - and put together in a totally different way. It is the creation of a person whose brain is already playing tricks on her - whose hands are almost too weak to hold a book and who is struggling to keep awake. To me it is a total miracle that she could have found words so beautiful, all on the one page opening of the book for it describes and sums up our pilgrimage together. So many of the themes are there, including the idea of ultimate freedom through the resurrection from the cancer-ridden body that had trapped her and imprisoned her.

David Helyar and I agreed on the order of service, and then I contacted all the people who were to take part. There were eighteen of them, and remarkably they were all available. One came back from holiday specially to do her part. It all fell into place so easily - a very complex service put together in a few hours with no snags at all.

The next day was the hard work of duplicating and posting the letters about Chris's death and funeral. Helen had to go back to work but Dave stayed till it was all done. Without him it would not have got done. I would have left it, I was so tired and emotionally drained. And then I was on my own - coming to terms with what had happened. I should have been taking the church meeting, but of course they managed without me. I thought of them, and they thought of me.

The next morning the telephone rang. It was Mabel - my Dad had had a fall - he had been taken to hospital. I didn't like the sound of what she said - he'd become unconscious and hit his head. He still seemed unconscious.

My brother was away on holiday in the caravan with just a contact telephone number for later in the week. I had to go - driving across London. I hoped I could manage it. I still felt in shock. I rang Sue and told her, and then off I went. The usual one and a quarter hours battle with London traffic to pick up Mabel and then off to the hospital. He had had a stroke, they said, and the first 24 hours were critical. He was semi-conscious, but apparently not paralysed. Later in the day he was more conscious, but not able to speak. Eventually I came away and drove back. Sue rang, and was relieved to know I'd made both journeys safely.

On Thursday, there were the usual early morning prayers with the local clergy, and I went. I was able to arrange with Dianna and Rosemary, Barry and Cecil, exactly what Chris had asked them to do in the funeral. It all seemed normal and yet unreal. Everyone was very sympathetic and helpful and most of them had a part to take at the service. The breakfast together was cheerful, but subdued. Chris had meant a lot to all of them.

Then Judith came to see me. It was to be the start of a very long series of meetings together over many months. Because of her contacts with us both, during Chris's illness the previous year, and right through the pilgrimage up to and including Chris's death, she had very valuable insights to share with me. Without her encouragement and her long periods of listening to me trying to sort out my thoughts, I could not have written this account. On virtually every occasion we have met, we have finished with prayers together led sometimes by her, sometimes by me. On this occasion it was just like a continuation of her visits to both of us, almost as if Chris were still there. She was a valuable link with Chris, and for that reason I wanted to hang on to her. I felt she understood, in a way no-one else did.

For the rest of the day I was making final preparations for the journey up north for Tim's ordination. It was quite a difficult operation, getting all the family up to Huddersfield for the great day, though of course everyone made their own arrangements.

So on the Friday I set off for Colchester, where I was to pick up Helen and Andy. It's not too difficult from Dulwich, using the M25 and the Dartford crossing, but it's pretty busy. We had lunch at Helen's hospital accommodation, and then set off up north. Some of the way was the same as Chris and I had travelled on our way to Iona and Callanish, but this time we were staying with Tim's friend Norman in Ashton-under-Lyne. It was good to see him, and he put on his usual wonderful meal. I felt perfectly able to enjoy it, and to enjoy the company of the three of them. It was a lovely occasion and we were all anticipating a happy time the next day. Of course, Chris should have been there - we had arranged some time ago that we would stay at Norman's the night before Chris's final goal.

The next day we were off to Huddersfield to see the new manse and the new minister! It was lovely to explore the house with its basement ready for all Tim's train memorabilia, and its attic which was to be Tim's study. The two middle floors were made really nice showing Rebekah's good choices, with wedding presents shown off to advantage, as well as some things I recognised from the Dulwich home! Rodney and Judith, Rebekah's parents, were there, and soon Dave and Ruth arrived, and Sue, Simon, and the children together with other friends of Tim and Rebekah's, and Thomas, her brother. It was a big family gathering - not what Tim enjoys! He was pretty uptight about all the arrangements at the church, and soon we were off there to get sorted out for the service. As we went in, we met my treasurer from Dulwich Grove - he'd come up for the day. I was so pleased.

David Peel, of Northern College, who was to preach, had arrived. He had sent me a draft of what he had to say earlier, and I had read it to Chris in the hospice. During the ceremony, Tim spoke about the influence Chris and I had been to him. It was mentioned in several places that Chris should have been there. At the laying on of hands Tim knelt and each in turn laid hands on him separately. It had been agreed with Chris that Dave would lay hands on him on her behalf - that was Tim's idea, but the congregation were not made aware of this. So I went first, then Dave, then other ministers. People found it very moving, and afterwards my brother said to Sue, "Did you see your mother laying hands on him too?" He felt very aware that it had happened - not through Dave, but in some other way.

Sue had to take the children out for a while, but while she was outside she felt the very strong presence of her mother telling her to go back into the service.

Others, too, felt Chris was there. Tim and I had no such feeling, in fact Tim's thoughts were to get it over with as quickly as possible! I just felt it was a happy day, surprisingly so, and I was pleased to meet so many friends. But to me, Chris had gone completely. It was only long afterwards that I learnt of my brother's experience, and I was very surprised and comforted. And I remembered that when Chris and I were talking to David Helyar about our hopes for Tim's ordination, she said that one way or another she was determined to be there, and David had said, "If not in body, then in spirit". What do we mean by these phrases we come out with? At this time I felt very upset in many ways, of course, but one thing troubled me greatly. I was not able to visualise Chris's face at all. I have always had trouble visualising, but I found this very difficult to bear, the one I had been with for 34 years of marriage, and no mental picture of her.

We travelled back on the Sunday, and I went via Colchester again to drop Helen and Andy off. That evening and night I was alone again - only the second time since Chris died. I felt a great longing to dream about her or to remember her clearly, but it was as if there were a great barrier, a solid wall that was impenetrable. She had gone completely.

I felt I must go down to the cottage again, but was not sure that I should go by myself. Dave took time off to go with me on the Monday evening and stay overnight. I was glad he came with me - I doubt I could have faced it on my own. There it was, surprisingly tidy, after we had left it five weeks before. Then, Chris had fallen in the bath, and I had eventually helped her out after a great struggle. It all came back to me. That night again Chris's face just wouldn't come into my mind just maybe a bit of an eyebrow, or her chin, but never her whole face.

But in spite of these problems with my imagination, the cottage was just as lovely as ever. I got a wonderful feeling about it just as before. I could come back and find its peace and feel the stress and burden of life lifting off me. I felt that here the memories would come back in time, and indeed, already were doing so, though not in a way I could visualise. We came back to Dulwich the next day and prepared for the funeral. People were coming and going and it's all a bit of a haze in my memory now. There was so much to do, there was no time to stop and reflect. And I felt strong enough to arrange that I would greet everyone as they came into the service. I wanted to meet everyone, and felt this was the only way to do it. I was amazed that so many people came, and was so glad to see them.

The funeral was very special - quite unlike a normal funeral. Chris's hand was on it all and it spoke of victory and resurrection. Tony Burnham's poem from the URC prayer handbook said just the right things:

"Take your canvas, God, and sketch on it a new life for me.
Shape me, style me, and shade me with your Spirit.
Paint over the old me with all my blemishes and flaws
And then with Jesus as your model
Draw my heart again and colour it with love.
Even if my body has been distorted by the passing years
And my face blotched and lined by life's experiences,
Brush my spirit with yours
Highlighting the beauty you pictured in me once before.
Paint me again as your child wide eyed with questions
Quick to speak all I know
Not worried by passing time nor stressed by duties undone
God, paint over the old me and draw me again
So that I can see the world from your perspective
Then, after growth and in wisdom perhaps one day
Someone will look and see in me your masterpiece .....
A portrait of the glory of Jesus."

And I could share in the prayers she had chosen

"We offer ourselves in our brokenness to be changed by your healing love and to be
instruments of your wholeness in our homes, churches and communities"

The prayer about the family was right too, but it hurt -

'Lord of the family you made us for one another because it is not good to be alone.
You blessed the links of marriage and kinship for our support and nurture.
Forgive us when conflict damages our closest ties
when we bring hurt and bitterness, rather than embracing forgiveness and life.
In home life and friendship let us love loyally, live honestly, serve lovingly and
welcome warmly.
Revive our families with your love, Lord, and we will praise you.'

She was no longer there to keep the family together. Would I be able to carry on where she left off? I felt broken and alone, though surrounded by my family. It hurt to walk into the church behind that coffin alone but I had to go through the hurt and bear it. *Take your canvas, Lord, and sketch on it a new life for me.* Had Chris chosen that with me in mind, or her? Or both? She was not there now to ask.

But I felt determined. Pain I might have, but no bitterness. Chris had lived a lovely life for her Lord, and I would do the same. I would try to let God work on me so that someone might one day see *'a portrait of the glory of Jesus'* as I had seen it in Chris. Somehow I had to get sorted out and begin to live again and not feel sorry for myself.

The high spot of the funeral, everyone agreed, was Simon's playing of *'The Swan'*. It was truly 'out of this world', and as I heard the music I imagined a beautiful swan gliding from the coffin across the curtains at the front of the church and away into freedom. I felt Chris had regained her beauty that the steroids, radiotherapy and cancer had destroyed, and that she was no longer confined. I felt so proud of her achievement. She has found her apricot tree for ever!

Epilogue

I have written this account because I have felt compelled to. I felt it was bursting inside me and had to come out. It has been a tremendous relief to put it onto paper. I have felt very strongly Chris's influence upon me to write it and much of it is Chris's, not mine. It is her testimony through me of her beliefs and her struggles. It is an explanation of how she could be so confident and serene as she faced her death, and a statement of her total belief in life beyond death.

I could not have written it without the patient listening of my family, of people at my church, of my bereavement counsellor at St Christopher's, and especially of Judith who has listened to me for hours and hours, time after time. I have had so much to off-load. Chris and I were never able to sit down and talk about the meanings of our pilgrimage, and I needed people to share with.

I also wrote a diary - I still keep it up - of events and feelings after Chris's death. Unlike C S Lewis's *A Grief Observed* the diary is not for sharing, but for helping me to recognise my emotions and thoughts, and try to sort them out from the confusion of the first few months. I found C S Lewis's book a tremendous help, not that I had thoughts like his, but the confusion was the same, my mind jumping in all sorts of directions apparently at the same time. As I read it and re-read it, I began to see the resurrection in it. For him, too, there seemed a great barrier between him and his wife after death, which gradually broke down a little. For a long time I did not dream of Chris, and could not visualise her or even feel any sign of her presence, but one night at the cottage I got what I had desired for so long. It was a feeling that Chris was very close, so much so that I felt if I opened my eyes I would see her, but there was nothing visual about it, nor was it a dream. I just knew it was her, reassuring me that in some way I could not understand she was alive beyond death. I felt so happy and content. For a moment the barrier had been drawn away. There have been precious times too at communion when I have felt very close to her, and sometimes I have resented having to preside because I have wanted to concentrate on that feeling. Yet maybe if I concentrated rather than having my mind on the liturgy the feeling would have evaporated - I don't know. Certainly, now I understand far more at communion what is meant by being united in Christ with those gone before.

Sometimes I want to hang on to these feelings, and I realise I cannot do this - it can be a kind of denial that Chris really died. And I understand more now Jesus's words to Mary in the garden on the first Easter morning, "Do not cling to me". Mary had to understand the reality of Jesus's death, and that resurrection life is something we can know of, but not share in, in any physical sense.

I have been faced with the question what do I do with the pilgrimage? And my answer is this book. But it is not the only answer. It is a part of me, and has become more part of me as I have written it down. Each period I have written about I have re-lived, entering into the various moods of these times in a quite remarkable way. I am sure I can help others more now because of my experience with Chris in pilgrimage together.

I was able to share with my church some of my thoughts and feelings during the church weekend away in October, two and a half months after Chris died. It had been planned for a very long time, and Chris had intended to be there with me. She had planned a visit during the weekend to our cottage at Sedlescombe, as it is only a few miles from Hastings, where we were staying together as a church. So the visit went ahead, and people were able to go around the cottage and its garden, seeing so much that reminded them of Chris.

Before they went to the cottage, I was able to talk to them about my bereavement and theirs, and of the pain and sorrow we all felt. I talked about us being wounded as church and minister by our bereavement. It was a Sunday, and I talked of the poster from Turvey Abbey which they would see, that Chris put up on Easter Sunday, 'He is risen'. It was an important time of sharing, and I was able to vocalise with them a problem that I was struggling with - "What am I going to do with my love for Chris?". Several people spoke to me afterwards thanking me for sharing and talking about this problem.

The church weekend away had been a 'goal' for Chris, as had a wedding in Germany, also in October. At first I felt I couldn't go, but then I decided to make the trip. It was a kind of living for Chris, attaining her goal for her, and it was an expression of my love for her.

Recently I attended the Seva Sadan Birthday Party in Birmingham, and again, it was a living for her as she had not been able to go to the previous one because of her illness, as I have recorded in this account.

To some extent now I can see that I can still love Chris by loving the things and the people she did. I have taken on the King's College Hospital chaplaincy and to some extent I do it because I love her. Her great interest in people for their own sake is something I admired and wish to copy.

And of course this book is an expression of my love for Chris. As I have written it, I have felt her hand on mine, and her thoughts flowing through me. I have almost heard her voice: "Tell people, John, what I discovered in my spiritual journey. I can't tell them myself, but I know you can act as my spokesman. Maybe it will be a help to someone".

As time rolls on, and I come to the anniversaries, to another Ash Wednesday, another Lent, Holy Week, Good Friday, Easter and Pentecost, I shall re-live, and seek to interpret again. At Easter I shall be able to identify more with Jesus's friends, bereaved and heartbroken, but coming to realise that life goes on beyond death. And maybe the message of Pentecost will show me the Holy Spirit leading on into the future, for as we both believed God planned this pilgrimage, so I believe that God has a plan for me here, and a plan for Chris in a way I cannot understand. We must leave it in God's hands in perfect trust.

I close with some words from the book of Isaiah, read at Chris's funeral, as she had planned.

> 'Here on Mount Zion, the Lord Almighty will prepare a banquet for all the nations of the world - a banquet of the richest food and the finest wine. Here he will suddenly remove the cloud of sorrow that has been hanging over all the nations. The Sovereign Lord will destroy death for ever! He will wipe away the tears from everyone's eyes, and take away the disgrace his people have suffered throughout the world. The Lord himself has spoken! When it happens, everyone will say "He is our God! We have put our trust in him and he has rescued us. He is the Lord! We have put our trust in him, and now we are happy and joyful because he has saved us".'

Isaiah 25: 6-9

ACKNOWLEDGEMENTS

Scriptures quoted from the *Good News Bible* published by
The Bible Societies/HarperCollins Publishers Ltd.,
UK © American Bible Society 1966, 1971, 1976, 1992 used with permission.

Passage from: *The Cross of Life* by Theodore Glaser,
© Evangelische Buchhife e. V., used by permission.

Prayer: *Take your canvas God* © 1989 Tony Burnham,
from *Say One For Me*, the Prayer Handbook for 1990,
published by the United Reformed Church in the United Kingdom.

AUTHOR'S ACKNOWLEDGEMENTS

This book was written and prepared for publication with the support of many friends. First I want to thank Judith Allford for her suggestion that I write it, and for her tremendous support as I did so. Without her it would not have been written. Then my thanks to Valerie Rivers for producing the original typescript from my illegible scrawl, and her encouragement to keep scrawling, and to Lesslie Newbigin for his insistence that it be published somehow!

My gratitude, too, to many people for suggestions during the editing stage, including Norman Hart and members of my family, and also to Gillian Smith for being willing to undertake the considerable task of editor.

It was wonderful news when I heard that the publications department of the URC were willing to accept the book for publication, and this was due in no small part to the enthusiasm of Carol Rogers, She and her team of helpers have worked so hard, in particular Sara Broughton who worked on the layout. The cover design and the line drawings were produced by Carol's daughter-in-law, Helen. My thanks to them all for offering to do the work.

Finally, may I thank my church, Dulwich Grove, for allowing me the time to write the book, and for being so understanding and supportive at this time.